AN UNDERSTANDING OF THE FUNDAMENTAL TECHNIQUES OF VOLLEYBALL

ROBERT E. HOWARD

Allyn and Bacon

Boston • London • Toronto • Sydney • Tokyo • Singapore

Illustrations by Scott Dye

Copyright © 1996 by Allyn & Bacon
A Simon & Schuster Company
Needham Heights, Massachusetts 02194

ISBN 0-205-16558-3

Printed in the United States of America

10 9 8 7 6 5 4 3   00

TABLE of CONTENTS

page #

Chapter 1: *INTRODUCTION*
History of Volleyball 1
General Rules of Play 3
Other Formats 7

Chapter 2: *OFFENSIVE PHILOSOPHY*
The Pass 9
The Attack 10

Chapter 3: *The FOREARM PASS* 15
Initial posture 16
Movement to the ball 18
Preparation to pass 23
The passing action 27
Contact with the ball 35
Follow-through 36
Key points 37

Chapter 4: *The OVERHEAD SET* 39
Initial posture 40
Movement to the ball 41
Preparation to set 47
The setting action 52
Contact with the ball 58
Follow-through 63
Backsetting 63
Jumpsetting 68
Key points 70

Chapter 5: *SPIKING* 73
The approach 74
The jump 84
The armswing 85
Contact with the ball 91
Follow-through and landing 93
Tipping the ball 94
Hitting quick sets 95
Key points 99

page #

Chapter 6: *OFFENSIVE DESIGN*
    Serve reception formations 103
    Basic systems of offense 106
    Offensive strategies 109

Chapter 7: *DEFENSIVE PHILOSOPHY*
    Serving 115
    Blocking 116
    Backcourt defense 119

Chapter 8: *SERVING* 121
    Initial posture 122
    The serving action 123
    Contact with the ball 129
    The underhand serve 130
    Key points 134

Chapter 9: *BLOCKING* 137
    Starting position 138
    Initial posture 139
    Outside blockers alignment 141
    Middle blockers alignment 145
    The blocking action 150
    Contact with the ball 153
    Follow-through and landing 154
    Key points 155

Chapter 10: *DIGGING* 157
    Positioning 158
    Digging spikes 160
    Playing behind the block 163
    Key points 165

Chapter 11: *DEFENSIVE DESIGN*
    Serving strategies 167
    Blocking strategies 168
    Basic defensive systems 170
    Special situations 173
    Transition 176

Appendix A: *GLOSSARY* 177

PREFACE

Much of the literature in volleyball tries to be all things to all people. It is only natural that an author and publisher would try to reach the largest possible audience. To that end, most books try to meet the needs of coaches, teachers, and players. They generally cover the whole spectrum from beginning play to advanced competition, from individual technique to team strategies, from drills and exercises to team training. Of course, all this must be accomplished in a limited space; otherwise, the book will be too expensive.

The broad coverage provided by most books limits the depth in which information can be presented. One of the distinctive features of this book is the depth of coverage given to the fundamental skills. Each skill is described in detail, and analyzed in comparison to other techniques.

People learn sports skills best when they 1) have a thorough knowledge of the movement pattern (the skill technique), and 2) have an understanding of why that particular technique will be effective. That is, learners need to know what to learn, and why. By limiting such areas as team drills, training, and advanced strategies, we are able to devote more space to developing such an understanding. We believe this orientation makes the material presented here valuable for both the student and the teacher, for both the player and the coach.

We do not pretend to have invented any new volleyball techniques. The techniques presented here are derived from many sources in contemporary volleyball knowledge:

1) They are representative of the current literature on volleyball skills.
2) They are among the techniques most often observed in quality play.
3) They are consistent with the findings of sports science research.
4) They are based on principles of biomechanical efficiency.

One thing that you may notice about this book is the informal manner of address. Because the book is written directly to students and volleyball players, statements are often directed to 'you' instead of 'the player'. We believe this makes the material easier to read, and much easier to understand.

ACKNOWLEDGMENTS

No work such as this emerges from a vacuum. This material has been greatly influenced by the writings that preceded it. To those authors, and other volleyball friends, I thank you for the contributions made to the understanding of volleyball presented here.

In addition, I would like to thank those who helped in bringing this project to completion. Without their contributions, the book could not have been written.

First and foremost, thanks to my Mom for all of her love and support.

A special thanks to Scott Dye, whose work and artistic abilities provided the images that illustrate this text.

Thank you to the following reviewers of the manuscript, whose knowledge and advice helped shape the presentation of this material:

Linda Halbert, UNC Charlotte
Barbara Drum, University of Maryland
Ann Lanphear, University of Maryland
Helen Timmermans, USC Columbia
Warren Hammer, University of Richmond
Angie Dilliner, Valdosta State University

And finally, thanks to the players and students that I have had the privilege to coach and teach, from whom I learned a lot.

INTRODUCTION

Volleyball is a sport that is played throughout the United States, and worldwide. Part of its popularity is that it can be played on many different levels, from pickup games to professional competition. It can be enjoyed by the the most intense competitor, as well as the casual participant.

History of Volleyball

The sport of volleyball was born in Holyoke, Massachusetts, in 1895, near the time and place that basketball was first played. William G. Morgan, at the time the physical director of the Young Men's Christian Association (YMCA), sought to develop an activity for the businessmen who frequented the YMCA. He envisioned a game that could accommodate a large number of participants, an activity that would not be too strenuous. The game that Morgan introduced (originally called mintonette) quickly developed into the sport of volleyball. In 1897 the playing rules were formally published.

Volleyball quickly spread across the nation. In the early years, the game took on many forms as it was adopted (and adapted) across the United States. There arose a need to consolidate and standardize volleyball play. The result was the formation of the United States Volleyball Association (USVBA) in 1928.

Volleyball became a common leisure activity for members of the armed forces. As U.S. servicemen were stationed abroad, especially in the years following World War I and II, they carried the game with them. Volleyball was introduced and embraced worldwide.

The growth of international volleyball mirrored the evolution of volleyball in the United States. Again, there arose a need to standardize and govern play, this time on the international level. In 1947, the organization currently known as the Federation Internationale de Volley-Ball (FIVB) was formed.

In 1964, volleyball was made the showcase event of the Tokyo Olympics. The Japanese Olympic teams not only dominated the competition, they revolutionized volleyball in the process. They introduced the forearm pass, and their fast-paced offensive and defensive strategies excited fans and generated enthusiasm for the game. The media attention surrounding the Olympics spread that enthusiasm around the globe.

The 1964 Olympiad is generally regarded as the beginning of volleyball's modern era. Since that time, the sport has continued to grow, both worldwide and in the United States. Every year, national teams from around the globe compete in international tournaments and leagues. Professional volleyball leagues now exist in Europe, Asia, and in North and South America.

In the United States, both men's and women's national teams have year round programs and training facilities. Volleyball is a primary sport in women's interscholastic and intercollegiate athletics nationwide, with many schools and colleges offering men's programs as well. Volleyball is used as a primary activity in physical education and intramural recreation. In addition, it occupies a solid position in many community and private sector recreation programs, serving enthusiasts of all ages and interests.

In its origins, the objective of Morgan's game was to keep the ball in play. Court dimensions varied according to the size of the building. Any number of participants, on either team, could play. An individual could contact the ball as many times as they wished, and any number of contacts were allowed for the team. Morgan's activity scarcely resembles volleyball as we know it today.

Today, the game has evolved into a fast paced, high energy activity, one in which speed and power are at a premium. The rules of play for volleyball have become highly defined. The major administrative groups which establish the rules governing volleyball play are:

1) Federation Internationale de Volley-Ball (FIVB) -
    the governing body for international volleyball.
2) USA Volleyball (formerly, the United States Volleyball Association) -
    the governing body for amateur volleyball in the United States,
    including the U.S. national team programs.
3) National Collegiate Athletic Association (NCAA) -
    the largest governing body for intercollegiate athletics.
4) National Association of Girls and Women's Sports (NAGWS) -
    the organization overseeing women's intercollegiate athletics.
5) National Federation for High School Sports -
    the governing body for interscholastic athletics.

Though different levels of volleyball play exist, each having their own governing body, the playing rules are fairly standardized throughout. FIVB rules set the standard for international competition. Many countries, including the United States, hope to compete on the international level. In order to prepare their players and teams to compete in the international arena, they adopt FIVB rules for their own country.

USA Volleyball, NCAA, and NAGWS rules are generally the same as FIVB rules. The most notable rule exception is that a more liberal substitution rule is allowed in women's intercollegiate play. Federation rules, with a few more exceptions, closely follow USVBA and NAGWS rules.

What follows is a general overview of the playing rules of volleyball. Keep in mind that rule changes occur with regularity. Also understand that many recreational programs modify these rules to suite their own requirements.

Basic Rules of Play

Play always starts with the serve, and play stops when the ball hits the floor, or when a rule violation occurs.
1) YOU WIN THE PLAY when:
    a)   the ball hits your opponent's court;
    b)   your opponent last touches a ball that lands out of bounds;
    c)   your opponent commits a rules violation.
2) YOUR OPPONENT WINS THE PLAY when:
    a)   the ball hits your team's court;
    b)   you, or a teammate, last touch a ball that goes out of bounds;
    c)   your team commits a rules violation.

Scoring

Generally, you can only score when your team serves the ball.
1) POINT - when the serving team wins the play, they score a point and continue serving.
2) SIDE OUT - when the receiving team wins the play, they gain the serve, but no point is awarded.
3) RALLY SCORING - Rally scoring is sometimes used in the deciding game of a match. In 'rally scoring', a point is scored on each and every serve.

A GAME   A team wins the game when they score 15 points. However, they must win by at least two points. Play continues beyond the 15th point until one team gains a two point advantage.

A MATCH   A volleyball match is a series of games.
1) 2-out-of-3 match - the first team to win two games wins the match.
2) 3-out-of-5 match - the first team to win three games wins the match.

The Court

The official volleyball court is measured in meters, rather than in the U.S. standard of feet and inches (fig 1.1, next page). Keep in mind that the line is part of the court. If the ball hits the line, it landed in the court.

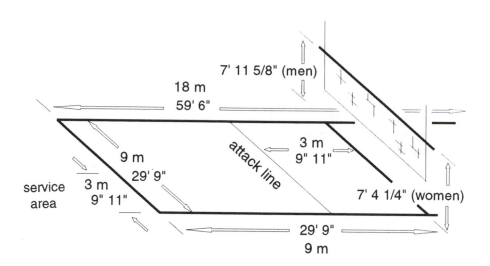

7' 11 5/8" (men)

18 m
59' 6"

9 m
29' 9"

attack line

3 m
9" 11"

service
area

3 m
9" 11"

7' 4 1/4" (women)

29' 9"
9 m

FIG 1.1: *court dimensions*

CEILING   What happens when the ball hits the ceiling?
1)   High school, middle school, and most recreational levels -
     a)   play continues if the ball comes down on your side of the court;
     b)   it is out of play if it comes down in your opponent's court, or hits the
          ceiling over their court.
2)   FIVB, USA Volleyball, and college play - the ball is out of bounds when it
     hits the ceiling. If the ceiling is below 23 ft, the rule is the same as above.

Players

LF = left front   CF = center front   RF = right front
LB = left back   CB = center back   RB = right back

     The line-up represents a specific serving
order. RB serves first. Whenever the team gains a
side-out, the players rotate clockwise, RF moving
to the service position (fig 1.2). On each
successive side-out, the rotation brings the next
player to the service position.

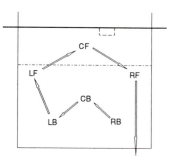

player positions: FIG 1.2

OVERLAP   Basically, once the server strikes the ball, players may move to any area on the court. Before the ball is served, however, each must be in their position relative to the players directly next to them.

For example (fig 1.3), LF must be in the shaded area: closer to the net than LB, and closer to the sideline than CF. Because LF is not directly next to CB, there is no overlap between them. LF can be farther from the net than CB.

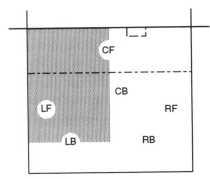

left front, non-overlap area
FIG 1.3

Ball Handling

TEAM BALL HANDLING   Team ball handling rules are fairly simple:
1)   a team is allowed only three (3) contacts;
2)   no player may contact the ball twice in succession.
3)   Exception - A blocker's touch DOES NOT count as a contact:
    a)   the team still has three contacts to use;
    b)   the blocker can hit the ball again, before anyone else contacts it.
    c)   Note: if the ball hits the blocker and flies out of bounds, the blocker would have touched it last, and the other team would win the play.

INDIVIDUAL BALL HANDLING   Ball handling violations occur when players mishandle the ball:
1)   LIFT - the ball visibly comes to rest in contact with the player.
2)   DOUBLE HIT - a player hits the ball twice consecutively. When setting the ball, for example, both hands must contact the ball at the same time.
3)   Exception: A double hit is legal when it is the team's first contact -
    a)   FIVB, USA Volleyball, and college - any first contact;
    b)   Federation (high school) - only when receiving a hard driven spike.
    c)   the player does NOT use finger action (the overhand technique). A double hit is never allowed when the player uses finger action.

Net Play

NET PENETRATION   When your opponent is hitting the ball across the net, you may reach across the net and block the ball so long as the offensive player contacts the ball first.
1)   FIVB, USA Volleyball, and college: players may NOT block a serve.
2)   Federation (high school): players are allowed to block a serve.

5

While you may reach across the net to block, you may not attack a ball on the other side of the net. When the ball is
1) ON YOUR SIDE of the net, you may attack the ball (fig 1.4a).
2) DIRECTLY ABOVE the net, either team may attack the ball (fig 1.4b).
3) ON YOUR OPPONENT'S SIDE of the net, you may NOT attack the ball (fig 1.4c); when you block, your opponent must contact the ball first.

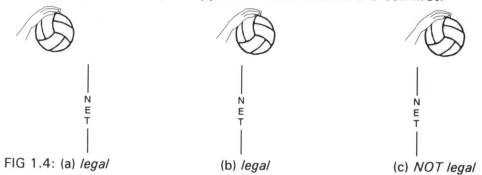

FIG 1.4: (a) *legal*   (b) *legal*   (c) *NOT legal*

NET CONTACT   Presently, players are not allowed to touch the net while the ball is in play. NOTE: a rule change getting serious consideration at higher levels would allow inadvertent net contact (contact that does not affect the play or create an advantage for the offending player).

CENTER LINE   The center line directly beneath the net separates your court from your opponent's.
1) A player may NOT contact the floor of the opponent's court with any part of the body other than their foot.
2) The foot may touch the opponent's court only so long as some part of the foot is still in contact with the center line (or is directly above the line).

Only front row players may block or spike. A backrow player is illegal when
1) BLOCKING:
   a) the backrow player's hand(s) must be higher than the level of the net;
   b) the ball must touch one of the blockers, though not necessarily the back row blocker.
2) SPIKING:
   a) The ball must be above the level of the net;
   b) the player must be standing in, or jump from, the attack zone.
Back row players may legally spike; but, their feet must be behind the 3-meter line when they jump.

Other Formats

Though 6-person volleyball is the norm, the game is often played in other formats. The playing rules are generally similar to 6-person rules. The following is a description of the various exceptions made for the other formats.

COED VOLLEYBALL   Teams consist of three males and three females. Males and females must alternate throughout the line-up; two males may not start next to each other, neither can two females.

If a team contacts the ball more than once, a female must touch the ball before it crosses the net. If, for example, a male were to receive the serve:
1)   legal ---- he passes the ball back across the net (legal, but not a good strategy).
2)   legal ---- he passes to a female, who sets a male spiker.
3)   legal ---- he passes to a male, who sets a female spiker.
4)   illegal -- he passes to a male, who sets a male spiker.
5)   legal ---- he passes to a female, who spikes the ball.
6)   illegal -- he passes to a male, who spikes the ball.

If a female receives the serve, the contact condition has been met; anyone can set the ball or hit it across the net.

When only one male is in the front row (this occurs every other rotation), a backrow male may come up to the net and block. This allows a team to always have two male blockers. The backrow blocker is still a backrow player in every other sense; they may not spike in front of the attack line.

DOUBLES and TRIPLES   Players in doubles and triples are not required to rotate. Right-side players, for instance, usually stay on the right for the entire game. Even though players do not rotate, each player serves in turn.

Players are allowed to cross under the net, so long as they do not interfere with their opponent's opportunity to play the ball. In addition, players may serve from anywhere beyond the end line.

Ball handling interpretations are a little different. Generally, the overhead setting must be cleaner. For example, the ball may not spin as much when you set; the setter must face the direction of the set (more so than in 6-person).

When digging a hard driven ball, a double hit is legal. In addition, a lift is allowed to some degree; you cannot catch the ball, but it does not have to bounce cleanly from the hands, either.

An open hand tip using the pads of the fingers is illegal. The tip must be a 'cut shot' off of the heel of the palm, or 'speared' with the finger tips.

7

OFFENSIVE PHILOSOPHY

Offensive philosophy revolves around spiking the ball. The pass (first contact) receives the serve, diminishes the ball's velocity, and redirects it to the net. The setter (second contact) delivers the ball to one of several hitters. The hitter then jumps and hits the ball forcefully down into the opponents court.

Although spiking is central to the game, no spike occurs if you cannot consistently pass the other team's serve. No spike occurs if you do not set the ball accurately to your hitters. You will find as you continue in the game that passing and setting are essential to your success.

The Pass

Generally, you should use the forearm pass to receive the first ball. However, you may use the overhead technique if the ball is moving slowly, such as a weak volley. It's usually not a good idea to receive a serve with your hands (using the overhead technique). It is not illegal, as some believe, just very difficult to do legally. For this reason, many leagues and instructional settings require that the serve be received using the forearm technique.

Serves, even soft serves, have too much force for the overhead technique to handle. If you receive the ball with your hands, the momentum of the serve usually pushes your fingers back, deforming your hand position so that the ball does not come out cleanly. Generally, you'll find that the forearm technique is much better suited to receiving serves.

LOCATION   Obviously, a good pass will fall within the range of the setter. In addition, the pass must be in an area where the offense can function effectively. Usually, you will need to pass the ball completely to the net. Very few offenses function well when the pass falls short of the net.

Many teams design their offense to operate slightly to the right of center. Other teams run their offense from the center of the net area. Very few teams, however, are effective when the pass goes to the left of center. Direct the pass to whatever target area is defined by your team's offense.

At instructional and non elite levels of competition, the right-of-center pass has distinct advantages. Many setters are stronger setting forward than setting back over their head. The right-of-center pass affords a shorter (and easier) backset and, of course, a longer front set. The right-of-center pass also makes it easier for your middle hitter to move in front of the setter, allowing the setter to see the hitter before delivering the set.

TRAJECTORY   Besides location, you should pass the ball through a specified trajectory. Usually this will be a fairly low trajectory. A good pass goes forward to the net, not up toward the ceiling. Generally, the pass should peak about 10-14 feet above the floor (fig 2.1).

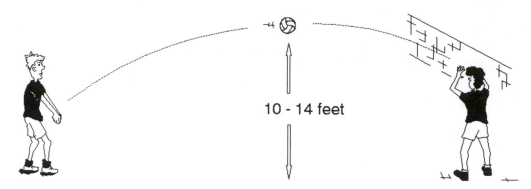

FIG 2.1: *pass trajectory*

A low pass travels primarily through the horizontal plane. The ball's momentum is easily transferred to the set, increasing the setter's strength. A high trajectory pass, however, gains momentum as it falls. The setter must first control the ball's downward momentum, using strength that could otherwise be used directing the set. This reduces the power and accuracy of the set.

You will often hear that a high pass gives the setter time to reach the ball. However, the additional motion that sends the ball upward makes passing more complex, less reliable. The high trajectory pass does, indeed, give the setter more time to chase the ball. Unfortunately, the setter often NEEDS more time.

In addition to being an easier technique to master, the low trajectory pass creates a tactical advantage for the offense. A low pass gets to the setter faster, providing a quicker attack and giving the opponents less time to react. The low trajectory also allows the setter to see the hitters and blockers while tracking the ball.

The Attack

The actions of the setter and the spikers are coordinated to bring about an effective attack. Both the hitter and the set are directed to the same attack location, and timed for the same set trajectory.

SET LOCATION   Set locations vary from team to team, based on each team's personnel and philosophy. However, there are general attack zones that are common to most offenses. The most basic locations are the areas near the net and sideline junctions.

10

Generally, the set should be about 2-4 feet away from the net, and within 3 feet of the sideline. Tape off a box, 2x3 feet, near the front corners of the court. NOTE: start the box about 2 feet away from the net (NOT at the net). These boxes are the typical attack areas; they are the target of most outside sets (fig 2.2).

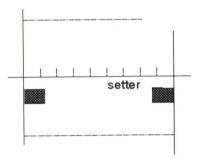

FIG 2.2: *set location boxes*

When the set is near the sideline, the hitters have more court to attack. Hitting down-the-line, the distance to the end line is 30 feet. Hitting cross-court, the distance to the opposite sideline is more than 30 feet (fig 2.3a).

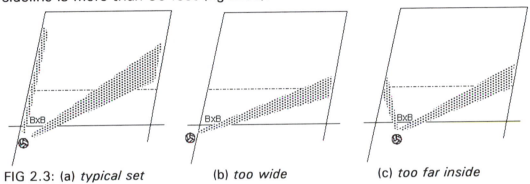

FIG 2.3: (a) *typical set*   (b) *too wide*   (c) *too far inside*

Setting the ball beyond the sideline eliminates the down-the-line spike, leaving only hit the cross-court shot (fig 2.3b). Setting the ball too far inside (5 feet or more) shortens the cross-court attack and reduces the down-the-line spike (fig 2.3c). Then, hitters must spike the ball at a sharp downward angle. This adds to the difficulty of the spike and brings the ball within easy reach of the blockers (the ball being lower when it crosses the net).

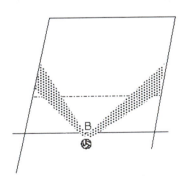

FIG 2.4: *middle attack*

The middle can also be an effective attack area (fig 2.4). The middle attack often allows you to hit against only one blocker instead of two. Of course, the opponent's outside blockers could move in and block alongside the middle blocker, in which case you lose that advantage

The middle set is usually more difficult to hit than is the basic outside attack. The sidelines are only 15-20 feet away. You must spike sharply downward to hit the ball in the court. And, you must turn the ball sharply to avoid the block.

DISTANCE FROM THE NET   Because middle attacks must be hit at a sharp downward angle, these balls are usually set closer to the net than outside sets. Generally, middle attacks are set 1-3 feet away from the net.

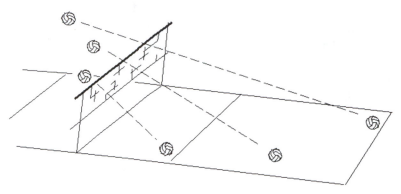

FIG 2.5: *spike trajectory*

Outside attacks should be set 2-4 feet away from the net, to the box described earlier. This is close enough for hitters to hit the ball at a downward trajectory (fig 2.5 above). Yet, it is still far enough away so they can hit around the blockers (fig 2.6a, below). It's close enough to hit with power, but far enough off so that there is room to swing.

Some hitters like their sets much closer to the net. Close sets can be hit downward at a radical angle, toward the 3-meter line (fig 2.5, above). This might be fun in practice and warmups (where blockers are usually not a factor). In actual games, however, close sets are easily blocked (fig 2.6b, below).

A set that is too far from the net will also be ineffective (fig 2.6c, below). From 5-7 feet off the net (or further), most hitters can only clear the net by hitting a flat trajectory spike (fig 2.5, above). The flat trajectory sends the spike deep into your opponent's court, giving the defenders more time to dig the ball.

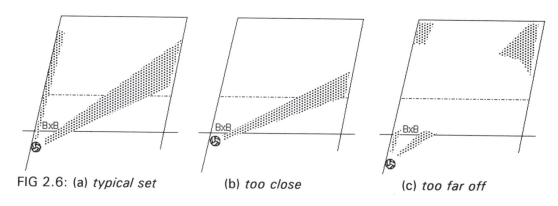

FIG 2.6: (a) *typical set*   (b) *too close*   (c) *too far off*

The attack will be most effective when the set is 2-4 feet away from the net. However, do not take this to mean that you should only hit perfect sets. Hitters should spike every set that they can hit into the court. It's much more effective to spike, even at 70%, than it is to volley the ball across the net.

ATTACK TEMPO   Tempo describes how fast an attack takes place. Basically, the height of the set determines the tempo of the attack. A high set takes longer getting to the hitter, so the attack develops slowly; thus, it is a slow-tempo attack. A low set gets to the hitter quickly, so the attack develops faster; thus, it is a fast-tempo attack.

The most basic set in volleyball is the high, outside set (fig 2.7). Because the set is high (peaking 8-12 feet above the net), the hitter can see where the ball is coming down as they start their attack, and make whatever adjustments are necessary. The success of the attack is less dependent on the set, and the setter.

basic high, outside set: FIG 2.7

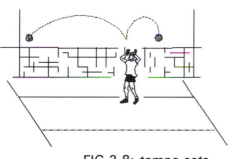

FIG 2.8: *tempo sets*

Balls that are set lower than the basic set are known as tempo sets (fig 2.8). Because tempo sets are lower, they get to the hitter much quicker. The hitter must start moving to the attack location before the setter delivers the ball. Your effectiveness, as a hitter, and the success of the attack is dependent on the setter.

1)   The setter must deliver the ball accurately, to the designated location.
2)   The setter must deliver the ball in timing with the hitter, through the designated trajectory.

Keep in mind that every attack is dependent on the accuracy of the initial pass. This is especially true of tempo-attacks. No matter how good the setter is, regardless of how good the hitters are, a team that passes poorly is rarely successful.

THE FOREARM PASS

The forearm technique is the most common method of playing the ball. Variations are used to receive serves and volleys, to dig spikes, and even to set. The forearm pass is arguably the most important skill in volleyball.

When passing the serve, there are a number of advantages to using the forearm, rather than the overhead technique.

1) You do not need such precise player-to-ball alignment; your ability to handle floating and high velocity serves is enhanced.

2) You contact the ball lower and, thus, later in the ball's flight; this gives you more time to reach the serve and make the pass, which increases your range.

3) The velocity of the serve does not easily deform the forearm contact surface, as it does the hand and finger contact surfaces of the overhead technique.

FIG 3.1: *the forearm pass*

The initial pass sets the stage for the entire offense. It is not enough for the setter just to be able to reach the ball. To be effective, a pass must allow all of the offensive options to be available. A poor pass limits the offense to one or two possible attacks.

Depth perception, hand-eye coordination, quickness, and technique are all factors contributing to a player's success in passing. Of these, technique is the easiest to learn.

Passing technique is largely a matter of moving to the serve or volley, and placing the arms in line with the ball. The passing action consists of little more than letting the ball rebound from the arms. A passer can use additional arm or leg movement to provide direction and distance to the pass. Such movements, however, may be unnecessary and could even reduce the passer's accuracy.

Often, a served ball has enough momentum so that the rebound alone will carry the pass completely to the net. When your arms form a firm rebound surface, you will need very little additional force (and, thus, little movement) during the passing action. The less movement there is in your passing action, of course, the less chance there is for error. Merely place your arms in line with the ball, and aim the rebound to the setter.

the passing platform:
FIG
3.2

This is the trademark of the rebound technique: very little arm movement during the passing action. You form a board-like platform with your arms (fig 3.2). Your legs transport the platform to meet the serve; your arms rebound the ball to the setter.

Initial Posture

Your initial posture should be similar to your passing posture. Think of how you look as you pass the ball (see above, fig 3.2). Start in a similar stance, with your board-like platform already formed. Maintain the platform as you move to the ball; then, when you reach the serve, you will be ready to make the pass. Over moderate distances (usually up to 10 feet), this is much more effective (and faster) than turning and running.

It takes too long to run to the ball . . . then prepare to make the pass. The time spent establishing your stance and platform, could be spent moving farther, covering more distance. You would increase your range, and you would have enough to pass with precise ball-to-body alignment more often. Your passing accuracy and consistency would improve.

16

Your initial posture should be different only in those areas where your movement would otherwise be restricted. For example, you cannot move very well with your elbows straight or your hands clasped together. Therefore, start with your hands separated and your arms bent slightly at the elbow.

THE STANCE   Wait for the serve or volley with your hips and shoulders directly facing the server (or the player volleying the ball across the net). Start in a balanced and stable posture (fig 3.3). Your first consideration is moving quickly.

Spread your feet a little more than shoulder width apart. Place your right foot forward; the heel of your right foot about even with the toes of your left. If you turn your toes slightly inward, your weight will shift forward, over the balls of your feet. In the left-to-right plane, distribute your weight evenly.

initial posture
FIG 3.3

Generally, your initial stance should be similar to that of a shortstop, or a basketball defender. Starting in a very low posture is no more advantageous than starting in a high posture. If you start too low, as many players do, you cannot gain speed without first rising. If you start too upright, your first step will be slow and short. Within these guidelines, use the starting posture that allows you to react and move most quickly.

THE PASSING PLATFORM   Relax your arms and extend them in front of your body, angled 30-45 degrees from vertical (fig 3.4). In an upright posture, your arms would be fairly close to your body. Bent forward at the waist, your arms would be farther away from your body. In each case, your arm angle will be the same: 30-45 degrees from vertical.

Start with your left arm near your left thigh, your right arm just inside your right thigh (see above, fig 3.3). This lowers your right shoulder, 1-2 inches, tilting your platform (and your pass) to the target area (right-of-center). Bend your arms slightly (15-30 degrees at the elbows) and you will improve your mobility.

30 - 45
degrees

arm angle
FIG 3.4

Your hands, at this point, should be approximately 18-30 inches apart. Shape your hands so that they are ready to clasp together. We recommend that you use the fist wrap. Loosely form a fist with one hand. Your other hand should remain open and relaxed, with the fingers curved. Point your thumbs down, comfortably pointed toward the floor.

Movement to the Ball

How you move to the ball (i.e., the footwork pattern you use) depends on how far away you are from the serve or volley. The slide-step footwork pattern will cover short distances (within 5 feet) and your body posture will change very little as you move. Using the crossover-step pattern, you can cover more distance (about 10 feet); though your hips turn, your upper body posture and your platform alignment will remain steady. Only when you have to go a long distance (more than 10 feet) should you turn and run to the ball.

Slide- and Crossover-Step Patterns

SLIDE STEPS (fig 3.5) From your initial position, identify where the serve or volley is going. Take a moderate length step with the foot nearest to the ball (your lead foot). Follow this step by moving your other foot (the trail foot) to within 6-12 inches of your lead foot. Immediately, almost before your trail foot touches down, step again with your lead foot.

FIG 3.5: *the slide-step pattern*

If, for example, the serve was to your left, your footwork pattern would be: left foot, then right and left (fig 3.5L). Stop your body's momentum and establish your passing stance as you take your last step. Be sure that your body movement places your arms in line with the ball; DO NOT reach for the ball.

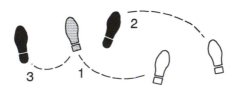 

FIG 3.5L: *moving to the left*   *moving to the right:* FIG 3.5R

CROSSOVER STEPS (fig 3.6)   When you have to move further, you will find the crossover pattern to be faster and more effective. Take a moderate length step with your lead foot, just as you do when using the slide-step pattern. Move your trail foot in front of and beyond your lead foot. This can be a short step, or a very long step, whatever you need to reach the ball. Immediately, step again with your lead foot. Usually, you take this step before your trail foot even settles down. The last two steps seem more like a hop onto both feet, but with a distinctive one . . . two landing.

FIG 3.6: *the crossover-step pattern*

If the serve was to your left, for example, your footwork pattern would be: left foot, then cross over and beyond with your right foot; immediately re-position your left foot (fig 3.6L). Slow your momentum as you take your next-to-last step; stop your body's movement and establish your passing stance as you take your last step. Again, DO NOT reach for the ball; your movement should bring your platform in line with the ball.

FIG 3.6L: *moving to the left*   *moving to the right:* FIG 3.6R

DURING MOVEMENT (using either slide or crossover steps)
When you move to the ball, keep your shoulders and platform nearly perpendicular to the flight of the ball (fig 3.7a), or as much as you can without

restricting your movement. DO NOT turn and face the ball. Many passers unnecessarily rotate their hips and face the ball when moving to pass (fig 3.7b). Then, they have to rotate their hips, or swing their arms, back to the target. This makes passing far more complex, and much less effective. Face where the ball came from, NOT the ball itself.

FIG 3.7a: *facing the server*   *facing the ball:* FIG 3.7b

A good place to contact the ball is between your waist and your knees. Measure the ball's flight and your movement so that you pass from this area. Move so that the ball would hit you in the left thigh.

In other sports, you commonly handle the ball up around the chest or shoulder area. This is where you catch and throw a basketball, football, and softball. Many inexperienced passers react to the serve similarly, and wind up with the ball coming at their chest. This is NOT an easy ball to pass. Play the ball at thigh level whenever possible.

While you are moving to the serve, lower your body to the level of the ball. DO NOT run to the ball, THEN try to get down low enough to make the pass.

You should be fluid and smooth as you move, not bouncing up and down as you take each step. Put rhythm into your movement. Practice your footwork with music; think of it as a dance, and your steps the choreography.

While you want to be fluid, not rigid, as you move to the ball, you should NOT let your arms swing freely, either. Carry your arms so that you can quickly form your passing platform when you arrive near the ball:
1) keep your platform angled 30-45 degrees from vertical.
2) continue to hold your arms slightly to the left of center;
3) move with your platform tilted toward the target area.

Keep your hands apart until you bring your outer arm in line with the ball. Moving with the hands clasped, of course, is very restrictive to your movement. Instinctively, you bend your arms trying to overcome this restriction. Then, as you near the ball, you have to re-straighten your arms. If you straighten your arms during the passing action, as often happens, you reduce the accuracy and effectiveness of the pass.

The Turn-and-Run Pattern

The crossover-step pattern may not generate enough speed for you to reach balls that are more than 10 feet away. In these situations, use the turn-and-run technique (fig 3.8). You can run faster using this pattern, but you still have to realign and prepare your platform once you reach the ball. Use the slide- or crossover-step pattern whenever possible. Use the turn-and-run to pass balls that you could not otherwise reach.

FIG 3.8: *the turn-and-run pattern*

As with the other patterns, take a moderate length step with the foot nearest the ball (the lead foot). As you take this step and recognize that the ball is far away, turn your hips toward the ball (unlike the other patterns) and begi to run. Continue running until you are near the ball.

FIG 3.8L: *moving to the left*

moving to the right: FIG 3.8R

DURING MOVEMENT (using the turn-and-run)
Assume a running posture:
1) Rise to a more erect stature as you run.
2) Let your arms fall to your sides and swing freely.
3) Bend your arms and bring your hands closer to your body.

Using the turn-and-run, you can take many steps, or just a few. Measure the length of your steps so that you take your next-to-last step (often termed the brake step) with the foot opposite your movement.
1) moving LEFT: brake with your right foot, then plant the left.
2) moving RIGHT: brake with the left foot, then plant the right.

During your last two steps, slow your momentum, gain balance, and prepare for the passing action (fig 3.9). Do this in one fluid motion. Do NOT stop . . . then gain your balance . . . then prepare to make the pass.

FIG 3.9: *turn-and-run, preparing to pass*

As you take your next-to-last step, brake your momentum. Rotate your body around this foot, much as a basketball player pivots on their pivot foot. Pivot far enough so that your hips and shoulders are again perpendicular to the flight of the ball.

As you take your next-to-last step and pivot around, bend your legs to adjust your platform to the height of the serve or volley. Raise or lower your body so that your platform is at the level of the ball. Bend at your knees; DO NOT bend from the waist. Stop your pivot and establish your passing stance during your last step.

22

Preparation to Pass

While you are moving to the ball, make any adjustments needed for the passing action. Remember, you want to be ready to pass when you reach the ball.

PASSING STANCE   Establish your passing stance as you take your last step (fig 3.10a). The placement of this foot should leave your feet spread wider than your shoulders; the lower the ball, the wider apart your feet should be spread (fig 3.10b). Balance and stabilize your body, keeping your weight forward on your front foot.

FIG 3.10a: *passing stance*

low passing stance: FIG 3.10b

Many different passing stances have been taught and used through the years. A current theory is that you will be most effective if you execute every pass from the same stance. It easier to learn and master one basic stance than learning to pass from several different stances. The right foot is always forward in the stance recommended for the rebound pass, from all positions on the court.

Place your right foot forward, with the heel of your right foot about even with the toes of your left. Keep your weight forward, toward your front foot. Your feet should be spread wider than shoulder width, so that you are balanced and stable.

It is especially important that your hips and shoulders are perpendicular to the flight of the ball. As you prepare to pass, you should be facing where the ball came from (the server, for example). This way, the ball always hits your arms squarely, rather than from an angle. DO NOT turn and face the ball itself.

For many years, passing with the outside foot forward was a common practice. Placing the outside foot forward turns the hips and shoulders toward the target area. The advantage is that the player is always passing straight ahead. The disadvantage is that the ball hits the arms from an angle, which affects the angle of the rebound. In addition, the player must learn to pass from the different stances used in different areas of the court.

PLATFORM   Before you reach the serve or volley, usually during your next-to-last step, position your arms to make the pass. DO NOT try to move your arms to the ball and pass all in the same motion. As you begin to move your arms in line with the serve, straighten your arms.

Many inexperienced players straighten their arms as they pass the ball. The action of arm straightening absorbs the ball's rebound from the platform. This causes the pass to fall short of the net. Players often swing their arms trying to regain the lost distance. This makes passing more complex, and more difficult. This is all unnecessary; just straighten your arms before, NOT during, the passing action.

Place the arm that is nearest the ball (your lead arm) in line with the ball's flight. The movement of this arm should be slow and controlled, giving you precise alignment. Your other arm (the trail arm) moves faster and arrives later, since it is farther from the ball. Join your hands as your trail arm arrives, using your lead arm to help stop its movement.

Once your lead arm is in line with the ball, join your hands. DO NOT join your hands, then move your arms to the ball. Moving the platform with your hands already joined is slow and imprecise.

Hand Clasp

The most important factor in joining your hands is forming an even passing surface for the ball to contact (fig 3.11a). When your platform is uneven, one arm is higher than the other (fig 3.11b). Usually, the ball bounces more strongly from the higher arm. Instead of a rebounding straight from your arms, the ball bounces off at an angle. The result is inaccurate and inconsistent passing.

even platform
FIG 3.11a   *uneven platform*
FIG 3.11b

FIG 3.12

There are many different ways you can clasp your hands, each affecting the passing surface that is formed. Make sure that you join your hands evenly. Joining the hands evenly is fundamental to forming an even platform. Generally, your arms will be even when (fig 3.12):

1)   your lower palm areas are directly side-by-side, and
2)   your thumbs are directly side-by-side and parallel.

The FIST-WRAP (fig 3.13) is a common method of joining the hands; it the hand clasp we recommend here. Start by forming a fist with one hand, while leaving the other hand open and relaxed.

fist-wrap: FIG 3.13

Join the hands by wrapping the open hand loosely around the fist. The wrap should be relaxed, but secure enough so that your hands do not separate when you contact the ball. Gripping tightly will tense your arms all the way up through your shoulders, making your arm movements stiff and clumsy.

The fist-wrap readily forms an even passing platform. Your lower palm areas naturally lie side-by-side, as do the thumbs. Gently rotating your forearms outward presents a hard, flat contact surface. The fist-wrap is an effective hand clasp, one that you can learn easily and master quickly.

The FINGER-CLASP (fig 3.14a) is a common method of joining the hands. It provides a strong hand clasp and, when done correctly, can provide a good passing surface.

The finger-clasp is formed by placing the fingers of one hand on top of the other hand's fingers. The palms lay side-by-side and face upward. Bring the thumbs together side-by-side, and press them downward against the fingers.

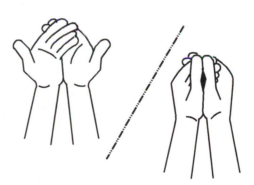

finger-clasp: FIG 3.14a

25

uneven finger-clasp
FIG 3.14b

The finger-clasp provides a wide, soft contact surface. However, the lower palm area of the top hand tends to slide up into the palm of the lower hand (fig 3.14b). This raises the top hand and forearm, making the passing platform uneven. The finger-clasp is an effective technique when the forearms are even. We do not recommend it here because it takes a long time to master and, until mastered, does not provide enough consistency.

The FINGER-INTERLACE (fig 3.15) is another hand clasp that forms a solid passing surface. Start with the hands and palms facing each other. Both hands should be open and relaxed, with the fingers separated.

Join the hands by bringing the palms together and lacing the fingers between each other. Make sure that you DO NOT grip tightly. You stiffen your arms all the way up through your shoulders when you grip tightly. This restricts the alignment of your platform with the ball.

finger-interlace
FIG 3.15

The finger-interlace forms a passing surface that is very similar to the fist-wrap. It is a very strong hand clasp: the ball does not easily knock the hands loose during contact. Unfortunately, the interlace exposes the fingers to injury whenever you fall to the floor, or when a ball bounces from the floor up into your extended fingers. Probably due to the risk of injury, the interlace is becoming less popular, its usage less common.

The PALM-CLASP (fig 3.16) is formed by gripping one hand in the palm of the other, with both palms facing upward. This grip presents the fleshy inner forearms to the ball, forming a wide, soft passing platform. However, because one palm is placed on top of the other, one forearm is usually higher than the other. The result is an uneven contact surface, and inconsistent passing.

palm-clasp: FIG 3.16

The palm-clasp is often used in recreational play, where participants have experienced little formal instruction. You'll also find that many players use this clasp in outdoor play, where the use of a softer ball compensates for the technique's deficiencies. The palm-clasp is the least recommended method.

The Passing Action

The passing action of the rebound technique (recommended here) consists primarily of the ball rebounding from your arms, and directing the rebound to your setter. Very little movement is required as you pass the ball.

An effective pass must be accurate in each dimension. The ball should travel through a specified trajectory. Its flight should be in a specific direction. It should go a precise distance. Your passing action directly affects each of these components.

Pass Trajectory

A good pass will generally have a low and forward trajectory. It will peak about 10-14 feet above the floor (3-7 feet above the level of the net). The two major factors affecting pass trajectory are:
1) the angle of the passing platform,
2) arm or body movements occurring during the passing action.

The recommended arm angle is about 30-45 degrees from vertical (fig 3.17a). This angle generally produces a pass that is forward, yet high enough so that the setter can reach the pass and deliver the set.

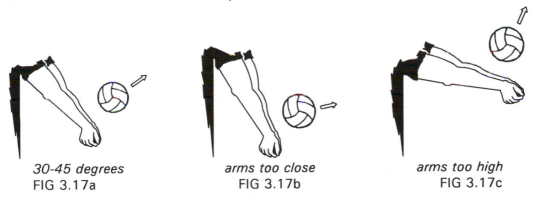

30-45 degrees
FIG 3.17a

arms too close
FIG 3.17b

arms too high
FIG 3.17c

If you hold your arms too close to your body, your platform will be nearly vertical. The result is a flat trajectory pass, one that is very low (fig 3.17b). If you hold your arms too high, your platform will be nearly horizontal. This will cause your pass to go up, rather than forward (fig 3.17c). This pass often sails high and falls short of the net.

Generally, you should not swing your arms as you pass. Keep your arms at the same angle throughout your passing action and your passes will have a consistent trajectory (fig 3.18), neither too high nor too low.

FIG 3.18: *no arm swing*

When you swing your arms during the passing action, you change your arm angle throughout the pass. This changes the trajectory of your pass, depending on where you contact the ball.

FIG 3.19: *swinging too late*

If you start the passing action a little too late, your arm angle will be nearly vertical, sending your pass low and fast (fig 3.19). If you start the action too early, your arm angle will be high (nearly horizontal), sending your pass upward and short of the net (fig 3.20).

FIG 3.20: *swinging too early*

Your arms should already be straight as you approach the ball. Keep them straight throughout the passing action. Gently point your thumbs and hands down, toward the floor; this helps straighten your elbows. Be careful not to point your thumbs down too strongly. This tenses your arms and shoulders, causing your movements to be rigid and awkward.

Bending your arms (at the elbow) during the passing action radically changes the angle of your passing platform. This generally causes your pass to go straight up . . . or worse, the ball flies back behind you (fig 3.21). DO NOT lift your thumbs or hands during the passing action. Usually, this causes your arms to bend, with predictable results.

FIG 3.21: *bending the arms*

Keep your torso comfortably upright throughout your passing action. Sometimes players arch their back as they make the pass (fig 3.22). Some players do this because the ball is too high above their waist, others do it out of habit. Arching the back during the pass sends the ball more upward and less forward, usually leaving the pass well short of the net.

FIG 3.22: *arching the back*

Leaning your torso forward some is beneficial, it helps keep your weight forward and gives you balance. DO NOT, however, bend forward at the waist to reach down for the ball; bend your legs instead. You lower the angle of your passing platform when you bend from the waist (fig 3.23). The more forward you bend, the more vertical your arm angle becomes, and the flatter your pass.

FIG 3.23: *bending from the waist*

There may be times when you need to bend from the waist to reach an extremely low ball. As you lower your torso, make sure that you adjust your arm angle so that your platform remains angled 30-45 degrees from vertical (fig 3.24). Keep in mind that bending from the waist should occur only when necessary, to play balls so near the floor they could not otherwise be reached.

FIG 3.24: *passing near the floor*

The rebound technique recommended here requires very little, if any, force from your legs. Primarily, your legs serve to stabilize your base of support. Pushing upward with your legs will cause your pass to go up toward the ceiling instead of forward to the net. Too often, your pass will be high and fall short of the net (fig 3.25).

FIG 3.25: *pushing upward during the pass*

Pass Direction

Using the rebound technique recommended here, you direct the ball by tilting your passing platform toward the target. Tilting the platform is a simple and effective method of directing the ball. It requires no additional movement of the arms or body during the passing action.

Think of your arms as a board. Place the board perpendicular to the ball's flight. Now, tilt the board (your arms) to the right. Which direction does the ball bounce? In the same way, tilting your passing platform directs your pass (fig 3.26).

tilting the platform
FIG 3.26

It is very important that you keep your hips and shoulders perpendicular to the serve or volley as you move to the ball. In addition, as you move to the ball and prepare to pass, keep your platform tilted toward the target.

Tilt your platform (the board) from your shoulders, NOT by turning your hands. Just lower the shoulder that is nearest the target (usually 1-3 inches). Since the target area is most often to the right of the serve's flight, you will generally lower your right shoulder. The farther to the right you want to pass the ball, the more you should lower your right shoulder.

31

Another simple way to tilt your platform is to contact the ball just outside your body's centerline. Place your arms to the left of your body's midline and your right shoulder will lower naturally. Generally, contact the ball between your midline and your left thigh to direct the ball to the right. The more to the right you have to pass, the more toward your left thigh you should contact the ball. DO NOT, however, line the ball up outside your leg; this makes passing much more difficult.

Not all passes, of course, are directed to the right. When you want to pass the ball straight ahead, do not tilt your platform at all. Keep your shoulders level and contact the ball near your body's midline.

Unless you specifically need to pass the ball to the left, which is rare, do not lower your left shoulder. In addition, DO NOT play the ball to the right of your midline. Lowering your left shoulder, of course, will tilt the platform to the left.

Poor passers often direct the pass by moving their platform during the passing action, either by swinging their arms or rotating their body. Both methods are very difficult to master, especially when passing the high velocity and floating serves used in competition.

Swinging your arms to direct the pass requires precise timing and alignment. Your arms, the ball, and the target must all be in the same straight line as you make contact. It is not easy to gain such precise alignment, especially as you move on to higher levels of play.

Think of swinging your arms as hitting a baseball. The passer is like a left-handed batter, with the setter out in center field (fig 3.27a). If they swing too late, the ball goes into left field (fig 3.27b); swing too early and the pass flies into right field (fig 3.27c). The setter, in center field, gets lots of exercise, but the offense is not going to be very effective.

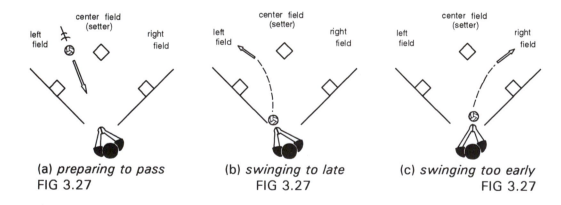

(a) *preparing to pass*
FIG 3.27

(b) *swinging to late*
FIG 3.27

(c) *swinging too early*
FIG 3.27

Rotating the hips to the target area during the pass is similar to swinging the arms. In the same way, timing and alignment are critical. Rotating too early sends the ball to one side of the setter; rotating too late sends the pass to the other side.

Tilting the platform is a more reliable way of directing the pass. Make sure that you move to the ball with your platform correctly angled and tilted. This way, you arrive near the ball with your pass's trajectory and direction already established. Merely place your arms in line with the ball: the ball rebounds to the target. With trajectory and direction already settled, the only variable in your passing action is distance.

Pass Distance

Using the rebound technique, the rebound alone is usually strong enough to send the ball all the way to the net. A firm passing platform and a stable stance are all you need.

Make sure that your weight stays forward, toward your front foot, throughout the passing action. Many players make the mistake of shifting their weight to their heels as they start the passing action (fig 3.28). This absorbs the ball, causing the pass to fall well short of the net.

FIG 3.28: *leaning back during the pass*

Swinging your arms is generally unnecessary . . . and risky. You increase the force of your passing action and, thus, the distance of your pass, when you swing your arms. How much force you add depends on how far and how fast you swing your arms. All too often, swinging your arms sends the ball over the net to your opponents.

There are, however, situations that require additional force (and distance) from your passing action. Slow-moving serves and volleys, for instance, may not have enough momentum to rebound all the way to the net. The following adjustments to your passing action will provide additional distance:
1)   move your hands forward (fig 3.29);
2)   shift your weight forward (fig 3.30).
Make each of these movements directly toward the setter's forehead. The movement should be forward, NOT upward.

FIG 3.29: *shifting the hands forward*

FIG 3.30: *shifting the weight forward*

Either of these methods can effectively add distance to your pass. Moving your hands forward (1) is the simpler of the two adjustments. Shifting your weight forward (2) maintains your platform angle. Whichever method you use, make sure that your platform moves no more than necessary, usually less than 6 inches. Keep the angle of your arms the same throughout the action; otherwise, you could change the pass's trajectory and distance.

Occasionally, a serve may be moving so fast that the rebound alone will carry the ball beyond the net. In such a case, you need to absorb the ball's momentum. Relax your hands, arms, and shoulders. This reduces the firmness of your platform, increasing the absorption of the ball's momentum and, thus, decreases the distance of your pass.

34

Contact with the Ball

You want your arms to form a flat, board-like contact surface; this is critical. When the ball contacts a flat surface, the rebound is straight and true. If your arms are uneven, the ball bounces from your arms at an angle. The same thing happens when the ball contacts a rounded surface, such as your wrist bone or hand area. Your pass could go anywhere.

Generally, you should contact the ball between your wrist bone and the bulge of your forearm muscles. Place a piece of tape around each forearm, about 2" above the wrist bone (fig 3.31). On every pass, try to make the ball hit on the tape. Feel when the ball contacts above or below the tape, then adjust on the very next pass.

FIG 3.31

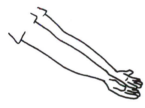

fleshy surface
FIG 3.32

Your forearms have a soft side and a hard side. To illustrate, try the following. Extend your arms out in front of you. Place your hands and forearms side-by-side, the heels of your palms touching. Turn your thumbs outward so that your palms are facing directly upward (fig 3.32). Notice that the forearms present a soft, fleshy surface.

Using this surface (the inner forearm area) to pass the ball gives you a wide soft contact area. The soft surface absorbs the ball's inertia and allows a longer contact between your arms and the ball. The theory is that increasing the length of contact increases your control of the pass.

However, because you absorb the ball's momentum, you decrease the distance of the ball's rebound. To compensate for the absorption, you must put more force (and, thus, more movement) into your passing action. This increases the complexity and difficulty of the passing action, costing you both accuracy and consistency.

Now, let's examine the hard side of your forearms. Again, extend your forearms out away from your body, side-by-side. This time, place your hands so that the palms are facing each other. Join your hands together palm to palm so that your thumbs are side-by-side (fig 3.33). Notice, now, that the forearms present a hard, bony surface.

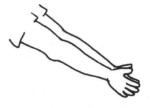

boney surface
FIG 3.33

This area (the top of your forearm) gives you a hard contact surface, but one that is narrow. The bony surface provides a solid rebound, one that will carry the ball a long distance. Unfortunately, the narrow contact surface often causes balls to be miss hit, and passes to be misdirected.

A combination of the bony and fleshy surfaces provides the most desirable contact surface. It gives a solid rebound while presenting a sufficiently wide contact area. This is the contact surface recommended here.

Again, extend your forearms out in front of you. As before, place your hands together with your palms facing each other. While keeping your thumbs side-by-side, gently rotate the top of your forearms outward about 45 degrees.

The "V" of your forearms forms a contact surface that is nearly symmetrical to the curvature of the ball. Now, the ball will contact both the bony and fleshy surfaces of your forearms. Your platform will have sufficient firmness without being too narrow. Notice, also, that the outward rotation brings your elbows and forearms closer together. This provides a more uniform passing surface along your forearm area.

Follow-through

Follow-through generally shows movement that occured during the passing action. Because the passing action requires little movement, there should be very little follow-through, if any. The presence of follow-through can be used to identify, and eliminate, any unnecessary movement occurring during the pass.

Key Points

INITIAL POSTURE
1. Stance
    a. Your right foot should be slightly forward of the left,
    b. feet spread a little more than shoulder-width apart,
    c. knees bent comfortably (45-60 degrees),
    d. hips and shoulders facing the server.
2. The passing platform
    a. Your arms should be angled 30-45 degrees from vertical,
    b. arms bent slightly (10-15 degrees) at the elbows,
    c. platform slightly to the left of your midline, tilted toward the setter,
    d. hands approximately 18-30 inches apart,
    e. one hand loosely forming a fist, the other open and relaxed.
3. COMMON ERRORS
    a. starting in too low a posture, or one that is too upright;
    b. starting with the arms too close to the body.

MOVEMENT TO THE BALL
1. Use the movement pattern best suited to the distance you must cover:
    a. 2-5 feet, use slide steps;
    b. 5-10 feet, use crossover steps;
    c. 10 feet or more, use the turn-and-run;
2. Maintain your passing posture as you move to the ball:
    a. keep your shoulders perpendicular to the flight of the ball (facing the server, NOT the ball);
    b. keep your platform to the left of center, tilted toward the setter;
    c. keep your arms angled 30-45 degrees from vertical;
    d. keep your hands separated.
3. Lower your platform to the level of the ball as you move:
    a. Bend your legs,
    b. DO NOT bend forward at the waist.
4. COMMON ERRORS
    a. turning to face the ball during movement;
    b. aligning the ball to the right of the midline;
    c. joining the hands during movement;
    d. reaching for the ball, rather than moving the body into position.

PREPARATION TO PASS
1. Stance
    a. The lower the ball, the wider your feet should be spread.

    b.   Your hips and shoulders should be perpendicular to the flight of the serve or volley.

2.   Platform

    a.   Straighten your arms, then

    b.   bring your arms in line with the ball, then

    c.   join your hands using the fist-wrap.

3.   COMMON ERRORS

    a.   joining the hands with the arms uneven;

    b.   holding the arms too close to the body;

    c.   starting the pass with the elbows bent.

THE PASSING ACTION

Basically, the ball rebounds from the arms to the setter. Very little movement is required in the passing action.

1.   Trajectory

    a.   Your arm angle should be 30-45 degrees from vertical.

    b.   DO NOT bend your elbows;

    c.   DO NOT arch your back as you pass.

2.   Direction

    a.   Tilt the platform toward the target area.

    b.   DO NOT swing your arms;

    c.   DO NOT rotate your hips.

3.   Distance is a factor of

    a.   the ball's velocity, and

    b.   the firmness of the platform.

    c.   DO NOT push upward with your legs;

    d.   DO NOT let your weight shift back on your heels.

4.   COMMON ERRORS

    a.   swinging the arms;

    b.   rotating the hips;

    c.   standing up during the passing action;

CONTACT WITH THE BALL

1.   Contact surface

    a.   Rotate your forearms comfortably outward, exposing the soft inner area of the forearms.

    b.   Contact the ball about 2 inches above the wrist bone.

2.   COMMON ERRORS

    a.   contacting the ball on or near the wrist bone;

    b.   letting the hands separate or shift during contact.

THE OVERHEAD SET

The overhead technique (fig 4.1) is a method of playing balls above chest level. The player handles the ball by cradling it in their hands, with the fingers and thumbs controlling the ball. A spring-like action of the wrists and fingers absorbs the ball's momentum, and reverses its direction. The ball is directed to the target by extending the arms while the hands are in contact with the ball.

The overhead technique provides more contact with the ball than does the rebound of the forearm technique:
1) The hands contact more of the ball's surface;
2) the hands are in contact a longer time;
3) the hands contact the ball for a longer distance.

The extended contact of the overhead technique makes it a more accurate method of handling the ball. Consequently, it is the preferred method of 'setting' the ball for the spike, and the primary skill that setters must develop.

FIG 4.1: *the overhead set*

Penetration to the Target Area

As a setter, your starting position is determined by a number of factors:
1) the offensive system being played,
2) the receive formation being used,
3) the team's rotation.

The starting posture is a matter of individual preference. The emphasis should be on moving quickly in a straight line. You know where you are going, and what path you are taking to get there. Being able to move in any direction is not generally required . . . not yet.

As soon as the opposing server strikes the ball, move to the area where your teammates are aiming their passes. Generally, this is right next to the net, and often it is to the right of center. You should move quickly to this position, arriving well before the passer contacts the ball.

Make sure that you are NOT still moving as the ball is passed. Wherever you are on the court, you must be balanced and stable when the ball is passed. If you are still moving, you will need to stop your momentum . . . regain your balance . . . then move in the direction of the pass. This is time consuming and limits your range tremendously. You could wind up setting balls with your forearms that you could otherwise reach and set with your hands.

Initial Posture

As you near the net, during your last two steps, establish your initial posture. Slow down and pivot to face the left sideline area as you take your next-to-last step. Stop and gain your balance during your last step.

As was the case with the forearm pass, your initial posture (fig 4.2) should resemble how you look when you actually set the ball. It is much faster (up to about 10 feet) to move to the ball in this posture than it is to move to the ball . . . then prepare to set.

Your initial posture should allow you to move quickly in any direction. Change only those aspects of the setting posture that would inhibit a quick start or slow your movement to the ball. For example, you can't move very fast running with your hands up around forehead level. So instead, start with your hands at about chest level, leaving your arms comfortably at your sides.

front view
FIG 4.2

STANCE   The placement of your last step should establish your initial stance. Place your last step so that so that your right foot is forward (6-12 inches) of your left, and your hips and shoulders are about 45-degrees from perpendicular to the net (fig 4.3), facing the left sideline. This allows you to see the whole court without moving your feet.

45-degrees: FIG 4.3

Generally, you should bend your legs enough to move quickly, but still remain comfortable. This varies a great deal from player to player, but it is generally about 30-45 degrees at the knees (fig 4.4). Some players move quickly from low posture; others move fastest from a more upright posture. Use whatever is best for you. Make sure that your weight is forward, toward the balls of your feet rather than back on your heels.

side view
FIG 4.4

HAND POSITION   Your hands should be at about chest level, your arms relaxed and comfortable. Form your hands and curve your fingers as they will be shaped when you contact the ball. Your thumbs, then, will be pointing back, toward your chest.

Your fingers, at this point, should be turned slightly upward. Do not relax your hands to the extent that your fingers are pointing down, at the ground. In addition, your hands should be separated no more than the width of the ball apart.

Focus your attention on the passer. You can get an indication of the pass's direction from:
1) the location of the ball relative to the passer's body;
2) the direction that the passer's hips and shoulders face;
3) the angle and tilt of the platform.

Movement to the Ball

Movement patterns for setting are similar to those discussed for the forearm pass in the preceding chapter. The primary difference is that setters must range farther (more than 10 feet) to reach the ball, and range farther more often. Setters find it necessary to use the turn-and-run movement pattern more often than passers.

As with passing, your movement pattern should allow you to move quickly to the ball, and arrive ready to make the set. It is very time consuming to move to the pass . . . then prepare your body for the set . . . then set the ball. If you combine these actions, you (as a setter) will have more time to run down bad passes, to align your body, to locate your hitters (and the opposing blockers), and to select the best attack option. You will increase your range, accuracy, and effectiveness.

As you pursue the pass, then, move with a body posture that is similar to your setting posture (fig 4.5), modified only where it would otherwise be restrictive. For example, the shape of your hands does not have much effect on movement speed. So carry your hands formed in the shape of the ball. This way, you will be ready to handle the ball when you reach the pass.

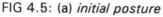

FIG 4.5: (a) *initial posture*   (b) *during movement*   (c) *setting posture*

Your arms, however, need to swing freely to counter the movement of your legs. Let them hang loosely at your sides while you move to the pass. You can move best with your elbows bent. So, bend your arms about the same as they will be when your hands are near your forehead. Moving to the ball, your hands will be somewhere near your chest. When you reach the pass, you only have to raise your hands about a foot and they will be in position to set.

How much can maintain your setting posture depends, to a large degree, on how far away the pass is. If the pass is only a step or two away, you can easily maintain the setting posture as you move to the ball. Your hips and shoulders, for example, can face the attack zone throughout the movement. When the pass is many steps away, however, you may have to run to reach the ball. You turn as you run, then turn back again when you reach the ball.

Movement patterns vary, therefore, depending on the distance you need to cover. Slide-step patterns are usually effective when the pass is within about 5 feet. Crossover steps cover more distance and are generally more effective, up to about 10 feet. The turn-and-run pattern produces the fastest movement speed, though extensive preparation is needed before you can set the ball.

SLIDE STEPS   The slide-step pattern (fig 4.6) is effective when you have a good pass. It allows you to keep both your hips and shoulders facing the attack zone as you move to the pass. In addition, your upper body remains postured and ready to start the setting action.

FIG 4.6: *the slide-step pattern*

Your first step (the lead foot) is usually a short or medium length step, depending on how far you have to move. As your lead foot settles to the floor, move your trail foot (next-to-last step) to within 6-12 inches of the lead foot. Measure the length of this step to bring your forehead in line with the pass.

Immediately, almost before your trail foot touches down, move your lead foot again and place it farther beyond your trail foot. This (your last step) controls your momentum and establishes your setting stance.

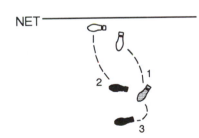

FIG 4.6L: *moving left*

You should take your first step with the foot nearest the pass. Generally this will be with your left foot when the pass is behind you or away from the net, followed by a right-left (fig 4.6L). However, when the pass is in front of you, take your first step with your right foot, followed by a left-right (fig 4.6R).

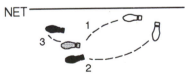

moving forward: FIG 4.6R

43

CROSSOVER STEPS   Setters more commonly use the crossover-step pattern (fig 4.7). As you move to the pass, your hips rotate a little more toward the ball, but your shoulders remain facing the left front attack zone. Your upper body remains postured and ready to start the setting action.

Again, take your first step with your lead foot. As this foot lands, move your trail foot in front of and place it beyond your lead foot. This step (your next-to-last) should be long enough to bring your forehead in line with the pass. Immediately, relocate your lead foot (last step) beyond the trail foot.

Often, your last step moves before your trail foot even touches down. For an instant, both feet are off the floor at the same time. However, there is a distinctive one-two sequence to the landing, next-to-last . . . then last.

FIG 4.7: _crossover steps_

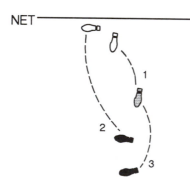

FIG 4.7L: _moving left_

As with the slide-step pattern, take your first step with the foot nearest the pass. Step with your left foot when the pass is away from the net or behind you, followed by a right-left (fig 4.7L).   When moving forward, step first with your right foot, followed by a left-right (fig 4.7R).

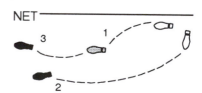

moving forward: FIG 4.7R

TURN-AND-RUN   Neither slide steps nor the crossover pattern are fast enough to use when the pass is more than about 10 feet away. The fastest way to reach and set such passes is to use the turn-and-run pattern (fig 4.8). Using the turn-and-run, both your hips and shoulders turn as you start to run. Then, when you reach the ball, you must turn back and face the attack zone.

The first step is similar to that of the other patterns. As you take this step, you should recognize that the pass is far away. Let your hips and shoulders turn as your other foot steps beyond your first step. Begin running to the ball.

When you run, let your arms swing freely, but continue to carry your hands near chest level. Your hands will be a little farther apart, but keep them formed in the shape of the ball. Let your body rise to a higher posture as you take longer strides. Continue running until you are near the pass.

FIG 4.8: *the turn-and-run pattern*

Measure your steps so that you take your next-to-last step with your right foot. This step should bring your forehead in line with the pass. Just before this step, begin lowering your body to place your forehead at the level of the pass. DO NOT bend forward at the waist to get under the ball; instead, lower your body by bending your knees.

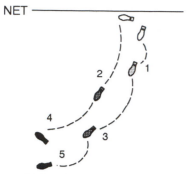

FIG 4.8L: *moving left*

Slow your momentum as you take your next-to-last step. Pivot around your right foot, bringing your hips and shoulders back around to face the attack zone. The placement of your last step should establish your setting stance and give you balance (fig 4.8L and fig 4.8R).

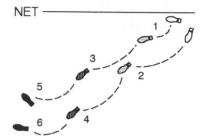

moving forward: FIG 4.8R

How much you rotate depends, to a large degree, on where you receive the pass. If you are setting from near the 3-meter line, you will not have to pivot much (fig 4.9a). When the pass is farther from the net, you will probably need to pivot more (fig 4.9b). Generally, you will pivot to face the left front attack area. However, you could pivot so that you face directly opposite the right front attack area, for a back set (fig 4.9c). Often, this involves less rotation and is the easier set.

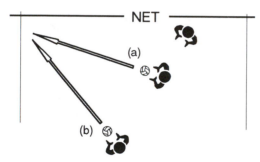

FIG 4.9a,b: *pivoting, front set*

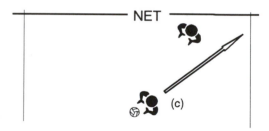

pivoting, back set: FIG 4.9c

ADVANCED VARIATION   As your skill progress, you can use a variation (fig 4.10, next page) of the turn-and-run to extend your range even farther. The variation is identical to basic pattern until you reach the ball and start to pivot.

Using the variation, keep your left foot off the floor as your body swings back around to the attacker. Deliver the set precisely when your shoulders face the attack area. After you deliver the set, let your left foot (previously, your last step) return to the floor and regain your balance.

Time your run so that your step, your rotation, and the start of your setting action take place as one fluid sequence. Contact the ball precisely as your rotation ends; DO NOT continue pivoting as you set the ball. This will cause your set to drift toward, or across, the net. It could also cause the set to be ruled illegal by the official.

The footwork pattern is very similar to the basic turn-and-run (see fig 4.8L and 4.8R, previous page). The difference is that your last step does not land until after you set the ball.

FIG 4.10: *advanced variation of the turn-and-run*

This variation can be very useful. However, the rotation and setting action timing is difficult to master. Even small mistakes can leave the set at the 3-meter line, or send it across the net. Therefore, use this technique ONLY when retrieving balls that could not otherwise be reached. Use the other footwork patterns whenever possible.

Preparation to Set

Regardless of which footwork pattern you use, you want prepare for the setting action while you move to the pass. During your movement,
1) as much as possible (depending on the footwork pattern), keep your shoulders facing the left front attack area;
2) carry your hands at about chest level;
3) your hands should be about the width of the ball apart;
4) keep your hands open, and shaped in the contour of the ball.

Maintain this posture as you move to the pass. Make the following adjustments before you reach the ball, during your last two steps:

1) raise your hands to forehead level;
2) turn so that your hips and shoulders are facing the attack area;
3) balance and stabilize your stance.

NEXT-TO-LAST STEP   Measure the length of your strides so that your next-to-last step brings your forehead in line with the pass. Lower your body so that your forehead is at the level of the pass as you take this step. If you took your hands out of the way, the ball should hit you between the eyes.

NOTE: Since setters generally face the left attack area when setting, many of the illustrations that follow are intended to be viewed "right-to-left", and are so denoted.

FIG 4.11 (view right-to-left): *bending at the knees*

Lower your body by bending at the knees, NOT from the waist (fig 4.11). Bending forward at the waist usually flattens the trajectory of the set (fig 4.12). Keep your trunk in a nearly upright posture and bend your knees instead.

FIG 4.12 (view right-to-left): *bending at the waist*

Moving to the ball, your hands should be formed in the shape of the ball and carried at chest level. When you approach the ball, just as you start to take your next-to-last step, begin raising your hands to a position in front of and slightly above your forehead (fig 4.13). Make sure that your hands stay near your torso as you bring them up.

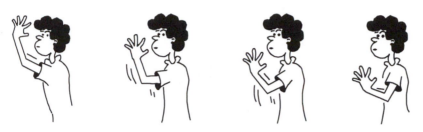

FIG 4.13 (view right-to-left): *raising the hands to forehead level*

Many players, especially inexperienced players, drop their hands to waist level as they move to the ball (fig 4.14). In preparing to set, they swing their hands up in an arc. The arc brings their hands up above their head, too high. Then, they have to return their hands back down to forehead level before starting the setting action. This lengthy movement is too complex, and unnecessary. It's much simpler just to bring your hands straight from your chest to your forehead.

FIG 4.14 (view right-to-left): *dropping the hands*

49

DO NOT let your hands drift apart as you raise them to your forehead (fig 4.15). Often, this causes one hand to apply more pressure than the other during the setting action. The set, then, goes to the left or right instead of straight ahead. Players also run the risk of bringing their hands back together too far apart, or too close together. Again, this will send the set away from the target area. In addition, this could result in a ball handling violation.

FIG 4.15 (view left-to-right): *hands too far apart*

Ideally, you should be facing the attack zone when you reach the pass. However, this is not always possible. Pivot as you take your next-to-last step, enough so that your hips and shoulders are again facing the left front attack area (as shown in fig 4.9ab, page 46), or facing directly opposite the right front attack area, aligned for a back set (as shown in fig 4.9c, page 46).

LAST STEP   As you take your last step, stop and gain your balance. The placement of this foot should establish your setting stance. When setting, you should have the foot that is closest to the net forward.
1)   This allows you to rotate your hips from the passer to the attack area without changing your stance.
2)   After delivering the set, your body will fall away from, rather than toward, the net.

For most setters, the foot closest to the net will be their right foot. Teams generally design their offense so that the setter always faces the left front attack area, and backset to the right side attackers. It is very rare that a setter faces the right sideline, even on a bad pass. Since you (as a setter) will be facing the left sideline, your right foot should be forward when you set.

FIG 4.16: *typical setting stance*

The heel of your right foot should be approximately even with the toe of your left (fig 4.16) or a little farther forward. Placing your foot too far forward would elongate your stance (fig 4.17). This restricts your weight shift. It also narrows your base of support, giving you poor stability.

FIG 4.17: *narrow setting stance*

Spread your feet a little more than shoulder width apart: the lower the pass, the wider your stance (fig 4.18). Make sure you distribute your weight evenly between your feet.

typical posture   low posture

FIG 4.18: *setting stance*

The Setting Action

Before you start the setting action (fig 4.19a),

1) your body should be balanced, with your weight evenly distributed;
2) your hips and shoulders should be facing the attack area;
3) your hands should be near your forehead;
4) your hands and fingers should be shaped in the contour of the ball.

setting posture
FIG 4.19a

During the setting action, the movements of your hands, arms, and body should all be directed through the same line. You do not want your legs pushing in one direction, your arms in another, and your hands in yet another. The direction of the set, both in terms of location and trajectory, depends on the coordination of these actions.

How far the set goes depends on the acceleration of your hands through setting action. The faster your hands are moving, the farther the ball goes. Long, high sets require a fast arm extension. When setting a short, low set, you can move your hands more slowly.

Time the set so that you start the setting action just before the ball reaches your hands (fig 4.19). Start by shifting your weight in the direction of the set. As your weight shifts, extend your arms and move your hands into contact with the ball. Continue driving your hands (and the ball) up and forward, sending the ball to the hitter.

FIG 4.19 (view right-to-left): *the setting action*

WEIGHT SHIFT   Just before your hands move to the ball, shift your weight in the direction of your set. Shifting your weight, of course, adds power

52

to the setting action. By gaining power from the weight transfer, you will need less power from your arms. Your hands, then, can move slower. This allows you to be in contact with the ball longer, which increases your accuracy.

To shift your weight forward, make a short, controlled push with your back leg (usually your left). Drive your center of mass directly through the intended flight of the set, forward and up (fig 4.20). Your weight will naturally shift onto your front leg. DO NOT push with your front leg; use the front leg to maintain your balance during and after your weight shift.

FIG 4.20 (view right-to-left): *recommended weight shift*

When you shift your weight, DO NOT push with both legs. This will drive your body straight up, vertically (fig 4.21). Instead of reaching to the outside attack area, the set is likely go straight up.

FIG 4.21 (view right-to-left): *pushing straight up*

When players push with both legs, the lower body may move backward, away from the direction of the set (fig 4.22). Obviously, this is not good.

FIG 4.22 (view right-to-left): *falling away*

Occasionally, you will see players trying to gain power by taking a step forward when they start the setting action. Taking a step is time consuming and limits the player's range. Often there is not enough time to get behind the ball, then take a step directly toward the attack zone. So, the player winds up setting while facing the ball, instead of the attack area. Often, the player also pikes their torso forward at the end of the step (fig 4.23). Bending forward at the waist, of course, lowers the trajectory of the set.

FIG 4.23 (view right-to-left): *stepping forward*

ADVANCED VARIATION   As your skill advances, you can gain additional power by letting your hips rotate during the weight shift (fig 4.24). Time your set so that you contact the ball just as your rotation ends. Then, the energy of the rotation is transferred to the setting action.

FIG 4.24 (view right-to-left): *rotate and set*

Make sure that your hips do not rotate beyond the attack area: rotate no more than 45 degrees and, usually, much less. Contact the ball just when your hips and shoulders face the attack zone (fig 4.25). DO NOT set the ball during your rotation. This often causes the ball to drift across the net, to the other team. In addition, if you rotate while in contact with the ball, your ball handling is likely to be ruled illegal by the official.

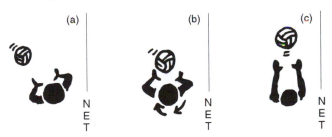

(view left-to-right)
rotate and set sequence: FIG 4.25

Similar to the turn-and-run variation, this is a very difficult skill to master; it can lead to many errors. Whenever possible, gain power from the standard weight transfer. Use this skill only when absolutely necessary, when you would not otherwise have sufficient strength to send the ball far enough, or high enough, to reach the hitter.

ARM EXTENSION   While your weight is shifting forward, BEFORE the pass reaches your hands, start your hands moving to meet the ball. Your hands should already be moving when they contact the ball. The momentum of your hands is transferred to the ball, providing power for the set. Generally, start your setting action when the ball is 1-2 inches away (fig 4.26). This will provide a good combination of power and control.

FIG 4.26 (view right-to-left): *recommended timing*

When you need power, such as making a long cross-court set, start your hands moving to the ball when it is about 2 inches away. Your hands will be moving faster, then, when you contact the ball, increasing the force of your setting action. However, the length of contact is less, reducing your control of the set.

Be careful that you DO NOT reach for the ball too soon (fig 4.27). If you start when the ball is 3 inches or more away, your arms will be nearly straight when you contact the ball. The length of contact will insufficient to provide much power or accuracy.

FIG 4.27 (view right-to-left): *starting too soon*

When the set does not require much power, such as a short set, let the ball get closer (about 1 inch away) before starting. Starting when the ball is almost in your hands increases the length of contact. Your hands will be moving slower, so you contact the ball longer. This gives more control, though not as much power. Short sets, however, do not require much power.

DO NOT wait until the ball touches your hands before starting the setting action (fig 4.28). When you do this, the ball settles in your hands, costing you both control and power. In addition, your set would probably be ruled illegal.

FIG 4.28 (view right-to-left): *starting too late*

During the setting action, your hands and arms should move in only one direction, forward. The action is never back toward your body. You absorb and reverse the ball's momentum by using a spring-like action in your wrists and fingers. This spring-like action is seldom a conscious act. It is a result of the forces acting while your hands are in contact with the ball.

DEEP DISH TECHNIQUE (NOT recommended)   You may see players, especially in the outdoor game, using a technique known as 'deep dishing'. The deep dish involves a conscious movement with the arms to absorb the pass's momentum (fig 4.29). The player bends the arms and brings the hands (and the ball) back toward the body. As the ball comes to a stop, the player reverses direction and moves the hands forward, sending the ball toward the attacker.

FIG 4.29 (view right-to-left): *deep dishing*

Because the arms absorb the ball's momentum, and because the forward setting action begins when the ball is stationary, no strength is needed from the wrists and fingers. The fingers merely relax and conform to the shape of the ball. The touch on the ball is very soft.

This technique does not provide a lot of strength. Much of the allowable contact is spent in the absorption phase, limiting the forward phase of the delivery. Should either the absorption or forward phase become prolonged, the set is likely to be ruled illegal by the official. Another disadvantage of this technique is its complexity; it is difficult to master. Timing is critical, as is the setter's 'touch' on the ball.

This technique is more suited to the outdoor 2- and 3-person game. Outdoor sets generally require less strength; balls are set lower and more inside. Outdoor rules also allow a longer contact with the ball. In addition, marginal passes are more likely to be set with the forearms in the outdoor game.

Contact with the Ball

FIG 4.30 (view right-to-left): *ball absorption*

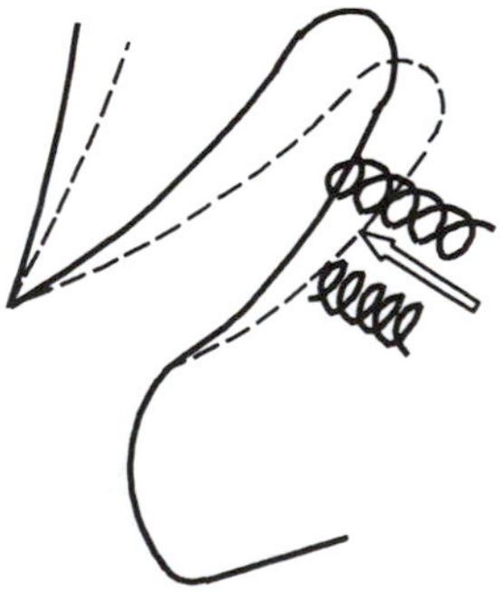

When your hands contact the pass (fig 4.30), the ball pushes against your fingers. Your fingers bend back (similar to compressing a spring), absorbing the ball's momentum and slowing its movement. When the ball stops, the tension in your hands causes the fingers to recoil (like a spring) back to their original position, reversing the ball's movement (fig 4.30a).

The strength of your spring-like action is directly proportional to the tension with which you shape your hands. Apply too much tension and the spring (your fingers) will be too stiff. The fingers will not bend at all;

spring-like finger action
FIG 4.30a

instead of pushing the fingers back, the ball bounces from the contact.

If you apply too little tension, the spring will be weak. Your fingers will only absorb the ball; there is no recoil. Find that range where you have soft hands, but also have a strong spring-like action.

As your setting skills advance, you can adjust the tension in your hands to your advantage. On sets requiring less strength, such as short sets, relax your hands a little more. Your hands will cradle the ball longer, giving you more accuracy. When you need additional strength, such as a long distance set, increase the tension in your fingers a little. Your hands will have a stronger spring-like action, giving you more power.

HAND SHAPE   During the setting action, your fingers encircle the rearward half and sides of the ball. Generally, you gain more control by contacting a larger area of the ball's surface. How well you handle the ball, then depends how you shape your hands. Ideally, your hands should be shaped similar to the contour of the ball.

When you set the ball, your palms should be NOT be facing forward. Nor should your palms be facing each other. They should be about half way in between: approximately 45 degrees from facing each other (fig 4.31).

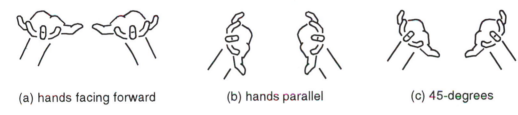

(a) hands facing forward   (b) hands parallel   (c) 45-degrees

FIG 4.31: *recommended hand position (c), 45-degrees from parallel*

Place your hands at chest level, with your fingers straight up. Your palms should be directly in line and facing forward (fig 4.31a). Now rotate your hands back so that the hands are parallel, with the palms facing each other (fig 4.31b). Half way between these two positions is the recommended alignment (fig 4.31c), approximately 45 degrees from parallel.

Again, place your hands at chest level, with this same alignment (45 degrees from parallel, fig 4.31c, above). Spread your fingers and curve them exactly as the ball is curved. This is how you should carry your hands as you move to the ball. Now, raise your hands to the level of your forehead (just as you would during your next-to-last step).

Your thumbs should be pointing back toward your nose or eyebrows (fig 4.32a). Your thumbs could even be pointing at each other without weakening your contact surface (fig 4.32b). But, your thumbs should NEVER be pointing forward (fig 4.32c).

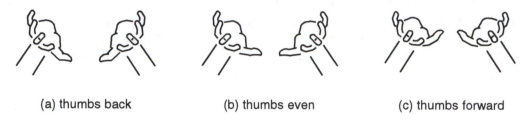

(a) thumbs back   (b) thumbs even   (c) thumbs forward

FIG 4.32: *keeping the thumbs back*

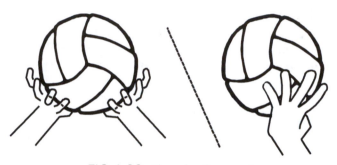

FIG 4.33: *thumbs forward*

You will see players, primarily at the recreational levels, who set with their thumbs pointing forward. To avoid hitting the thumbs, they naturally contact the ball higher in the hands (fig 4.33). Only the finger tips, then, control the ball. Compare the size of this surface with the preferred contact surface (fig 4.34).

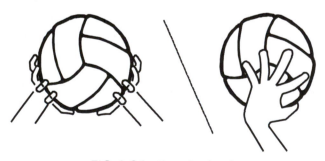

FIG 4.34: *thumbs back*

Repeat the process of forming your hands at your chest, then bring them to forehead level once again. Keeping your thumbs back, point your fingers straight up, vertically. If you were to set the ball with your hands in this position, your set would be flat and, usually, too low (fig 4.35a).

Now, (again, keeping your thumbs back) tilt your hands so that your fingers are almost horizontal (fig 4.35b). If you were to set with your hands in this position, your set would probably go straight up.

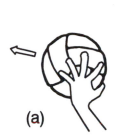  

(a)   (b)   (c)

FIG 4.35: *tilt of the hands*

You will have the best results if your hands are about half way between the two positions. Generally, your middle and index fingers should be about 30-45 degrees from vertical (fig 4.35c). This will place these two fingers approximately perpendicular to the intended flight of the set.

CONTACT SURFACE   Cradle the ball in your fingers and thumbs; DO NOT let the ball touch your palms. You should contact the ball primarily with your index and middle fingers, along with your thumbs. Your ring and little fingers have only limited contact with the ball. They resist any lateral forces occuring during your set, forces that would cause the ball to leave your hands at an angle, rather than straight. Like the walls of a river levee, they 'channel' the ball in the direction of your setting action (fig 4.36).

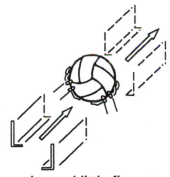

ring and little fingers
FIG 4.36

(a)   (b)

FIG 4.37: *finger curve*

Curve your fingers exactly as the ball is curved (fig 4.37a). Then, you will contact the ball all the way down to the second knuckle your fingers, and the first knuckle of your thumbs. If your fingers are curved too much, only the finger tips will contact the ball (fig 4.37b). This, of course, is not very effective.

61

Spread your fingers and thumbs comfortably (fig 4.38a). Spread them enough so that you cover a large surface of the ball, but not so much that your hands become stiff. If you spread your fingers too much (fig 4.38b), your fingers will be rigid, causing the ball to the ball will bounce from your hands. If you spread your fingers too little (fig 4.38c), you will contact a smaller area of the ball's surface.

(a) spread comfortably

(b) spread too much

(c) not enough

FIG 4.38: *spreading the fingers*

FIG 4.39

During the setting action, your hands should remain shaped in the contour of the ball (fig 4.39). DO NOT rotate your hands outward as you extend your arms (fig 4.40, below). As soon as your hands rotate, the fingers begin to lose contact with the ball. This, of course, weakens the setting action.

Players often do this when they use too much wrist action to set the ball. Instead, let your arms direct and power the set; your wrists should adjust so that you maintain steady contact with the ball.

FIG 4.40

Make sure that your hands are no farther apart than the width of the ball. If your your hands are too far apart,

1)   one hand may exert more pressure on the ball;
2)   the ball might hit one hand before the other;
3)   it could settle deep in your hands, contacting the palms.
     From the time you reach the net, until you finish your setting action, keep your hands about a ball's width apart.

Follow-through

When you shift your weight onto your front foot, it is natural that you should take a step forward (with your back foot) to maintain your balance. Note that this step occurs after the setting action is complete and the ball is in flight to the hitter. DO NOT take this step while you are handling the ball.

At the end of your arm extension, your hands will naturally rotate outwardly, but only a little. This occurs AFTER the ball has left your hands. Such follow-through does not affect the flight of the set. Generally, your follow-through should leave your arms and index fingers pointing toward the ball.

Once the ball is gone, your job as a setter is not complete. Mentally, you should evaluate the trajectory and location of your set. You should also make note of the defenders' reaction to your offensive options. However, DO NOT stand in one spot and evaluate your play. Make your mental notes while you move to your area of hitter coverage.

The Backset

The backset is a method of delivering the ball back over your head to a location behind you. This is an important skill for players at all levels. The backset allows you to deliver the ball to either side of the court regardless of which way you are facing. Since most systems operate with the setter always facing the left front attack, backsetting is an essential skill for setters.

As with all sets, accuracy and consistency are the most important qualities of a good backset. Your backset should be as hittable as your front set. At higher levels, setters conceal the set direction until the last possible moment. This is only valuable, however, when the set is deceptive AND accurate. You gain nothing by deceiving the blockers if the set is unhittable.

When making a backset, your initial posture, movement to the ball, alignment, and hand position are identical to a regular set. The differences in the backset occur after you reach the ball, during the setting action. Modify only your setting action.

As you reach the ball, turn so that your hips and shoulders face directly opposite the attack location (usually the right front attack area). Many advanced setters decide where to set at the last moment. They face the front set and then rotate to the backset just before starting the setting action. This makes the setting action more deceptive, but also more complex and more difficult. Until you have mastered the skill, you would be better off lining up the backset as you approach the ball.

As with the front set, start your setting action by shifting your weight from your back leg to your front. As you start the setting action (fig 4.41):

1) Push with your front leg so that your hips move upward, NOT forward; your body does not move backward, either, it rises straight up.

2) Extend your arms upward, in a line parallel to your upper back (almost straight up).

3) Arch your back, directing your arm extension back over your head, sending the ball directly behind you.

FIG 4.41 (view left-to-right): *the back set*

ARM EXTENSION   As you start to move your hands to meet the ball, arch your back. If you did not arch, your hands would go straight up, vertically. It is your back arch that changes the arm angle and sends the ball back over your head, behind you (fig 4.42).

Your back arch (how much you arch) determines the set trajectory, and how far behind you the ball goes. The farther you are from the hitter, the more arch you need. In typical situations, where you are only 7-10 feet away from the attack location, you will need very little back arch. Beware of arching too much; this gives the set a flat trajectory and, often, sends the ball beyond the sidelines.

back arch: FIG 4.42

FIG 4.43 (view left-to-right): *pulling the hands back*

Some players try to backset by pulling the ball back over their head with a short, rearward motion of their hands (fig 4.43). Other players turn their thumbs forward, trying to get their hands more underneath the ball (fig 4.44). These weaken the setting action and cause you to be very erratic. Remember, it is the back arch, not the movement of your hands, that sends the ball back over your head.

FIG 4.44 (view left-to-right): *turning the hands under the ball*

TIMING   Timing is critical to the strength and accuracy of a backset. When timed correctly, the sequence will be one smooth, continuous movement. When the ball is near your hands, within 1-2 inches: shift your weight, then arch your back and extend your arms.

65

FIG 4.45: *simultaneous arm extension and back arch*

Your back arch and arm extension should occur AT THE SAME TIME (fig 4.45). Then, the back arch adds energy to the action of your arms. This gives your backset additional power and distance. Be careful that you DO NOT arch your back first . . . THEN start your arm extension (fig 4.46). This will reduce your power, and 'telegraph' the backset.

back arch . . . then arm extension: FIG 4.46

If you start your setting action too soon, you will have to reach up to contact the ball (fig 4.47). This reduces the length of your contact, limiting your ability to direct the ball back over your head. You lose both control and power.

FIG 4.47: *starting too soon*

BALL ALIGNMENT   Your forehead should be directly in line with the pass. A common error in backsetting is lining the ball up over the head, instead of the forehead (fig 4.48). The contact point, then, is too high, which weakens the setting action. Often, the set will be too low to hit.

FIG 4.48: *ball directly over the head*

FIG 4.49: *contact too far in front*

If the ball is too far in front of your forehead, you will have a difficult time directing it back over your head (fig 4.49). This will also be the case if the ball is below forehead level (fig 4.50). You'll find that many of these sets go straight up, coming down near you instead of your hitter.

FIG 4.50: *contact too low*

67

The Jumpset

As with the backset, the jumpset is a fundamental skill for setters at any level. It allows you to set balls that otherwise would sail over your head. At higher levels, the jumpset can increase your range and to speed up the offense.

The jumpset is not very different from a regular set. Your movement to the pass, the setting action, and hand position are he same. The difference is that you jump up to elevate your forehead to the level of the pass (fig 4.51). Use the jump set for a tactical advantage; DO NOT jump into the ball to gain power.

FIG 4.51 (view right-to-left): *the jump set*

TIMING   Time your jump so that you start your setting action just before the peak of your jump, but while you're still ascending. If you did not set the ball, it should hit you in the forehead. Think of it as jumping to hit a header in soccer. Then, when you start the setting action, the ball would be 1-2 inches from your forehead and hands.

Timing is critical to an effective jumpset. If you jump too soon, the ball may be out of your reach. Also, your body could start to descent before you deliver the ball. When this occurs, you lose power and distance on the set. Jumping late adds power to the set, but little additional height.

THE JUMP   As you approach the ball, during your next-to-last and last steps, lower your body and prepare to jump (fig 4.52, next page). Bend your knees about 90 degrees or less. From this position, jump forcefully so that your forehead is elevated to intersect the pass. Make sure your jump brings your forehead completely to the ball.

FIG 4.52 (view right-to-left): *the jump*

Most players use their arms when they jump, gaining additional lift by swinging them upward. Make sure that you keep your elbows bent (about 90 degrees) and your hands shaped to make the set from the time you take your next-to-last step until you are airborne. When you jump and drive your hands upward, then, you will naturally bring your hands up near the forehead. You will be ready to set as you leave the ground; in the air, you will not have to re-position your hands before handling the ball.

FIG 4.53 (view right-to-left): *the jump setting action*

THE SETTING ACTION   The setting action for a jumpset (fig 4.53) is identical to that of a traditional set. The keys for success are the same:
1) rotate your body so that you are facing the attack area;
2) start the setting action when the ball is 1-2 inches from your hands;
3) contact the ball just above, and in front of, your forehead;
4) drive your hands (and the ball) through the intended trajectory of the set.

69

Key Points

INITIAL POSTURE
1. Stance
   a. Your right foot should be slightly forward of the left,
   b. feet spread about shoulder-width apart,
   c. knees bent comfortably (45-60 degrees),
   d. hips and shoulders about 45 degrees from perpendicular to the net.
2. Arms and hands
   a. Your hands should be held near chest level,
   b. elbows bent slightly about 90 degrees,
   c. hands approximately a ball's width apart,
   d. hands shaped and fingers curved in the contour of the ball.
3. COMMON ERRORS
   a. hips and shoulders facing the passer (parallel to the net);
   b. hands held down at waist level.

MOVEMENT TO THE BALL
1. Use the movement pattern best suited to reach the pass:
   a. 2-5 feet, use slide steps;
   b. 5-10 feet, use crossover steps;
   c. 10 feet or more, use the turn-and-run;
2. Maintain your setting posture as much as possible:
   a. keep your shoulders facing attack location;
   b. keep your hands at chest level,
   c. keep your hands separated the width of the ball,
   d. keep your hands formed in the shape of the ball.
3. Move your body so that your forehead is in line with the pass:
   a. Bend your legs,
   b. DO NOT bend forward at the waist.
   c. DO NOT reach for the ball.
4. COMMON ERRORS
   a. turning to face the ball during movement;
   b. dropping the hands to waist level during movement;
   c. intercepting the pass above or below forehead level.

PREPARATION TO SET
1. Stance
   a. The lower the ball, the wider your feet should be spread.
   b. Make sure that you ar facing the attack location, or directly opposite for a backset.

2. Arms and hands
   a. Bring your hands directly to your forehead,
   b. keep your hands shaped and fingers curved in the contour of the ball.
3. COMMON ERRORS
   a. turning the thumbs as they move into setting position;
   b. bringing your hands too high above forehead level, or too far below.

THE SETTING ACTION
1. Weight shift
   a. Shift your weight from your back foot to your front foot;
   b. your hips and torso should move in the same line as the trajectory of the set;
   c. DO NOT push straight up, or fall back on your heels, during the weight shift.
2. Arms and hands
   a. Move your hands toward the ball when it is 1-2 inches from your fingers.
   b. Move your hands in a straight line, through the ball and toward the point where the set should peak.
   c. Keep your hands and fingers shaped in the contour of the ball throughout the setting action.
   d. DO NOT let your hands rotate outwardly during the setting action.
3. COMMMON ERRORS
   a. standing up during the setting action;
   b. moving the hands to the ball too soon, or too late;
   c. using too much wrist action during the set.

CONTACT WITH THE BALL
1. Primary contact
   a. is with the index and middle fingers, and the thumbs;
   b. contact should be along the fingers down to the 2nd knuckle, and the 1st knuckle of the thumbs.
2. The ring and little fingers
   a. resist any lateral forces given the ball;
   b. they 'channel' the ball toward the hitter.
3. COMMON ERRORS
   a. setting with the hands too far apart;
   b. using only the finger tips to contact the ball.

FOLLOW-THROUGH
1. Follow-through should be made directly toward the peak of the set.

SPIKING

When spiking, you jump into the air, then forcefully strike the ball downward. The spike consists of three components: the approach, the jump, and the arm-swing. The approach takes you to the set; the jump elevates you into the air; and your swing delivers force to the ball. Do not, however, think of these as three separate actions. These should merge into one smooth, fluid sequence.

FIG 5.1: *spiking the ball*

A team's formation and rotation dictate where each player starts on the court. Usually, one or more of the front row hitters are included in the receive formation. When you, as a hitter, are also responsible for receiving the serve or volley, make sure that you pass first . . . THEN, move into position to spike.

Too many hitters pass poorly, or fail to pass at all, because they are too anxious to spike. Only when the pass is assured can you move into hitting position, to your approach point. Ideally, you should be at your approach point BEFORE the setter delivers the set.

The Approach

The approach is the footwork pattern used when moving to the set. Your approach should build speed and power for the jump. The last two steps of the approach (the next-to-last and last steps) are known as the transition phase. The transition converts your running speed (horizontal) into upward thrust (vertical). This adds additional inches to your jumping height. The transition should also align your body for the armswing.

You will find many different approaches used in volleyball. Some of these approaches are very effective, others are not so effective. Some approaches serve a highly specialized function, such as hitting quick sets, while others provide more range and versatility. Approach patterns are generally classified by the number of steps taken, the transition phase, or the sequence of steps:
1) NUMBER of STEPS -
    a)   the quick 3-step,
    b)   the traditional 3-step,
    c)   the 4-step.
2) TRANSITION phase -
    a)   the 'step-close', and
    b)   the 'step-hop'.
    c)   NOTE: the transition phase of both the step-close and the step-hop count as two (2) steps.
3) SEQUENCE of STEPS -
    a)   the 'standard approach', and
    b)   the 'goofy-footed approach'.

The 3- and 4-step patterns are most the common. Additionally, a 5-step pattern is occasionally used by hitters passing from deep in the court, or far from the attack location. The 5-step pattern is little more than a series of running steps leading to the 3- or 4-step pattern.

Generally, you would be wise to learn more than one approach pattern. This will make you a more versatility (and more valuable) hitter.

74

THE QUICK 3-STEP (fig 5.2)   A quick 3-step pattern (sometimes called a 2-step approach) is often used for hitting fast-tempo attacks, especially 1st-tempo sets. Because the approach is so short, you will usually start only about 7-11 feet from the attack location.

FIG 5.2: *the quick approach*

Start with your feet in a comfortable stride position, one foot slightly forward of the other. Which foot you place forward depends on where the pass comes from. Regardless of whether you are right-handed or left-handed, if the pass comes:
1) from the left of your body, place your left foot slightly to the rear, opening your hips to face left.
2) from the right of your body, place your left foot slightly forward, opening your hips to face right.

right-hander
FIG 5.2R

Your 1st step should be a short, controlled step. Usually, you will take this step as the passer contacts the ball. No matter which foot is forward, take your 1st step with the foot of your non-hitting hand.

Time the pass before taking your 2nd step. The 2nd (next-to-last) step should be strong and powerful. It can be a long step, or a short step, whichever covers the remaining distance to the attack location. Your last step (3rd) follows immediately.

left-hander
FIG 5.2L

The pattern is:
1) RIGHT-HANDERS (fig 5.2R) - short left (rhythm), right-left.
2) LEFT-HANDERS (fig 5.2L) - short right (rhythm), left-right.

THE 3-STEP APPROACH (fig 5.3)   The basic 3-step is a fairly common approach. It is a simple and effective pattern, one that you can learn easily and quickly. The 3-step often serves as a foundation for learning the other patterns.

The 3-step is a very fast approach; this allows you to judge the early flight of the set before you start moving. Using the 3-step, your approach point is fairly close to the net, usually within 9-14 feet. As an outside hitter, this limits your ability to adjust to inaccurate sets, especially those which are set away from the net. Your ability to pass from deep in the court, and then hit balls close to the net, is also limited.

FIG 5.3: *the basic 3-step approach*

The step sequence for the basic 3-step approach is the same as for the quick 3-step. Because the basic 3-step starts farther from the net, your 1st step must be longer and more powerful.

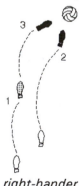

right-hander
FIG 5.3R

Start with the foot of your non hitting hand well back of your other foot. Take your 1st step with this foot, usually just after the setter releases the ball (depending on your quickness and the height of the set). Your 1st step should be strong and powerful; it builds speed and covers distance.

Your 2nd (next-to-last) step continues to build speed. This step should take you to the ball. It can be a short step if the ball is set off the net, or a long step if the set is far away. It is followed immediately by the last (3rd) step.

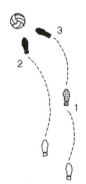

left-hander
FIG 5.3L

The pattern is:
1)   RIGHT-HANDERS (fig 5.3R) - strong left, right-left.
2)   LEFT-HANDERS (fig 5.3L) - strong right, left-right.

THE 4-STEP APPROACH (fig 5.4)   The 4-step approach is the most common pattern in volleyball, and the most highly recommended. It allows you to build more speed than the 3-step approach, and increases your range. Because the 4-step pattern covers more distance, you can start farther from the net, usually 12-17 feet. This allows you to adjust to poor sets, especially when the ball is set off the net. It also allows you to pass from deep in the court and still hit effectively.

You can easily learn the 4-step approach from the basic 3-step pattern. Just take a short rhythm step, followed by the basic 3-step approach. It is like getting a rolling start in a drag race.

FIG 5.4: *the 4-step approach*

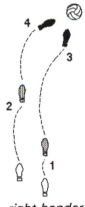

right-hander
FIG 5.4R

Start with your feet in a comfortable stride position; either foot can be forward. Take your 1st step with the foot of your hitting hand, usually just before the setter delivers the ball.

Take your 2nd step just after the setter contacts the ball (sooner or later depending on your quickness and the height of the set). This should be a powerful step, one that builds speed and covers distance.

Continue to build speed as your 3rd (next-to-last) step takes you to the ball. Your last (4th) step follows immediately.

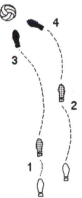

left-hander
FIG 5.4L

The 4-step pattern is:
1)   RIGHT-HANDERS (fig 5.4R) -
      short right (rhythm), strong left, right-left.
2)   LEFT-HANDERS (fig 5.4L) -
      short left (rhythm), strong right, left-right.

Approach Transition

STEP-CLOSE TRANSITION (fig 5.5)   The step-close is the most common transition, and the one generally recommended. In game conditions, you often have to adjust your approach to reach the set, even when you are just hitting basic sets. This is especially true when you are hitting tempo attacks. The step-close transition gives you the flexibility to do this.

The step-close transition has a distinctive 'one . . . two' sequence to the placement of the feet: your next-to-last step, then your last step.
1)   RIGHT-HANDED hitters - your right, then your left,
2)   LEFT-HANDED hitters - your left, then your right.

FIG 5.5: *the step-close transition*

When you take your next-to-last step, plant with the heel first. Your forward momentum then causes your foot to rock from the heel to the toe area. This heel-to-toe rocking action starts your jump. Your last step follows immediately, moving forward even before your next-to-last step touches down.

Your last step plants later than your next-to-last step. Since your body continues moving forward until your last step lands, this foot plants closer to the net. Placing your last step (foot of the non-hitting shoulder) closer to the net turns your non-hitting shoulder towards the net. Your shoulder alignment is similar to throwing a ball.

Plant your last step so that your foot points slightly inward. Contact the floor only with the ball of the foot; your heel does not initially touch the floor. This gives you greater body control during the transition, and more control during your jump. Place your foot so that your feet spread about shoulder width apart. Having your feet too close together affects your balance; placing them too far apart restricts your jumping ability.

STEP-HOP TRANSITION   We do NOT recommend the step-hop, though it was popular at one time. Some believe that its strong heel-to-toe rocking action transfers more running speed to your jump. There has been little research to prove whether this is true. Regardless, the step-hop provides little stability, and its use has steadily declined over the years.

The transition of the step-hop (fig 5.6) is actually a hop onto both feet before jumping. You enter the transition phase by pushing off with one foot while your other foot (the next-to-last step) moves forward. The push-off foot then rushes forward (last step) to catch up with your lead foot, allowing both feet to touch down simultaneously. Your heels contact the floor first, then you rock forward from your heels to your toes. This heel-to-toe rocking action starts your jump.

FIG 5.6: *the step-hop transition*

Of course, in game conditions you will not always be able to take a straight ahead approach when you hit. The step-hop transition limits your ability to move to the set from one direction, then spike in another. This is a major limitation at all levels of volleyball play. At the developmental levels, especially, you'll find yourself adjusting to the sets far more often than you would like.

Approach Footwork Patterns

THE STANDARD APPROACH   The standard approach, along with the step-plant transition, is almost universally recommended. This is the approach illustrated earlier for the 3-step (fig 5.3, pg 76) and 4-step (fig 5.4, pg 77) patterns. The sequence of the last three steps is what characterizes the standard approach:
1)   RIGHT-HANDED hitters - left, right and left.
2)   LEFT-HANDED hitters - right, left and right.

The standard approach allows you to jump with your non-hitting hip and shoulder forward, toward the net. This places your hitting shoulder back, similar to a throwing position. You will be ready to hit when you leave the ground; you will not have to realign during your jump or in the air. Your movements will be fluid, and your spiking action efficient.

GOOFY-FOOTED APPROACH   As you might guess from its name, the goofy-footed approach is NOT highly regarded. At the higher levels of play, goofy-footed hitters are a rarity. At the lower levels, however, they are more common than you might think. Many players fall into this pattern until they learn another approach.

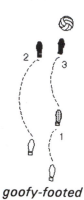

You are goofy-footed if your last three steps are:
1)   RIGHT-HANDED hitters (fig 5.7R) -
    a)   step-close: right, left and right
    b)   step-hop: right, hop to both feet.
2)   LEFT-HANDED hitters (fig 5.7L) -
    a)   step-close: left, right and left
    b)   step-hop: left, hop to both feet

goofy-footed
right-hander
FIG 5.7R

goofy-footed
left-hander
FIG 5.7L

The goofy-footed approach naturally turns your hitting shoulder toward the net. This is similar to stepping with your right foot to throw a ball (right handed); it limits the strength of your throw, and your accuracy as well. In the same way, a goofy-footed approach limits your spiking power and accuracy.

Goofy-footers often try to realign their hitting shoulder:
1)   they rotate their body during the jump;
2)   they twist their torso once they are in the air;
3)   they shorten their last step, so that their feet land side-by-side;
Each of these adjustments makes hitting more complex, and more difficult. Shortening the last two steps shortens their approach, restricting their range. Twisting during the jumping action takes energy from their jump. Twisting also moves the hitting shoulder away from the attack, an action that must be reversed as they swing. This complicates and weakens the spiking action.

Approach Distance

Spike approaches are designed to cover a general distance. This distance will not be the same for every player. One player's 4-step approach might cover 11 feet. Another player, one with longer legs or greater speed, might cover 14 feet using the same 4-step approach.

Once you have learned an approach pattern, you need to determine the distance that you will normally cover using that approach. The following is one method of measuring your basic approach distance, and marking your approach point (that point where you start your approach).

Start at the 3-meter line, facing AWAY from the net. Without the ball, approach and jump 20 times (moving towards the end line). After each landing, mark the spot from which you jumped. After the 20th jump, find and mark the center of all your jumps. Measure the distance back from the center back to the 3-meter line. This is the average length of your approach.

Most offenses try to set the ball 2-4 feet away from the net. You want to jump just behind the ball, about 3-5 from the net. Let's say that your approach covers 9 feet. If you want to jump 3-5 feet from the net, your approach point should be about 13 feet from the net (or, about 3 feet behind the attack line). If your approach covers 12 feet, start about 16 feet from the net (or, about 6 feet behind the attack line).

Many players start much too close to the net. They mark their approach point from the net, as though the ball will be set right on top of the net. You see these hitters jumping and hitting right next to the net in practice. Then, in a game, they run under sets that, otherwise, would be very easy to hit. Do not make this mistake; mark your approach according to where the sets are being directed, NOT the net.

Obviously, not all sets go where they are aimed. Often, you will need to adjust according to the set. It is best to adjust your approach. DO NOT run to a spot and, then, try to adjust your jump to reach the ball. Trying to adjust in the air, after you jump, is even more difficult and less effective.

Adjust your approach by increasing or decreasing the length of your strides. DO NOT change the number of steps that you take. DO NOT alter the sequence of those steps.

Develop the ability to vary your approach. Do hundreds of approaches without the ball. Do these at full speed and jump high. Each time, go to a different spot; learn to hit from different locations. Then, when you get a poor set in a game, you will be able to adjust naturally.

Ball Alignment

When you spike, time the set so that you hit the ball at your highest reach. In addition to a high contact, you want to hit the ball at a downward trajectory, so that it stays in the court. Line the ball up accordingly during your approach.

Adjust the length of your approach so that when you are in the air and ready to swing, the ball will be 6-12 inches in front of your hitting shoulder (fig 5.8a). At this point, the arc of your armswing is downward, yet the contact point remains high.

FIG 5.8a

You will not be effective if you contact the ball much farther in front of your shoulder (12 inches or more, fig 5.8b). The arc of your armswing is increasingly lower as your hand moves forward: the farther forward the ball, the lower your contact. In addition, the arc is increasingly downward: the further forward, the more downward your spike. The result, all too often, is that you hit the ball into the blockers . . . or worse, into the net.

FIG 5.8b

You will also be ineffective if the ball is behind your shoulder (fig 5.8c). The arc of your arm-swing would then be upward: the further behind your shoulder, the more upward. Generally, this results in a spike with an upward trajectory, often sending the ball out of bounds.

There is a time, however, when you should line the ball up directly above your shoulder. When spiking deep sets, 6-8 feet or more away from the net, most hitters need to hit a flat trajectory to clear the net.

If the set is off the net, line the ball up directly above your hitting shoulder. At that point, the arc of your arm-swing

FIG 5.8c

will be horizontal, giving your spike a flat trajectory. Make sure that your wrist-snap gives the ball enough top-spin so that it sinks after crossing the net. Without top-spin, the balls you hit hard will go out of bounds; only your weakest hits will stay in play..

Preparation to Jump

Time the set so that you approach and jump in one continuous sequence. You will lose momentum and power if you plant your feet . . . then bend your legs . . . then jump. Prepare for the jump as you enter your approach transition (see fig 5.5, pg 78).

Just BEFORE YOUR NEXT-TO-LAST STEP LANDS, begin bringing both arms back behind you. Your arms are the trigger for the jumping action. If you pull them back too soon, your body wants to jump before you set your feet. Obviously, this is not good. If you pull your arms back too late, however, you will not be ready to jump when your last step touches down. You stop . . . then you jump. This takes valuable inches from your jump.

AS YOUR NEXT-TO-LAST STEP LANDS and your last step moves forward,
4)   continue pulling your arms back behind you;
5)   lower your torso comfortably (no more than 30-45 degrees);
6)   keep your head up so that you can continue tracking the set;
7)   bend your legs to a knee angle between 90 and 110 degrees.
The ideal knee angle for jumping varies from player to player. Some hitters jump higher by bending deep (more than 90 degrees), dipping closer to the floor. Others jump better by not dropping so deep. The 90-110 degree knee angle is a good general range. From there, find out what YOUR best range is.

AS YOUR LAST STEP LANDS, your non-hitting hip and shoulder should be forward, closer to the net (fig 5.9). Your shoulders should NOT be parallel with the net; instead, they should be
1)   ON-HAND side, 30-45 degrees from parallel with the net,
2)   OFF-HAND side, 15-30 degree angle from the net.

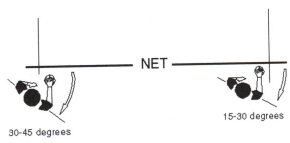

FIG 5.9

The planting of your last step starts the jumping action. You will be aligned and ready to hit as you leave the ground.

The Jump

By jumping, you increase your hitting height. The higher you hit the ball, of course, the more effective you can be as a hitter. In addition to elevating your body, the jump should also leave you postured in the air, ready to swing.

AS you plant your last step, three actions occur simultaneously (fig 5.10):
1) rapidly swing both arms forward and upward;
2) lift your torso, arching your back slightly;
3) push explosively with both legs.

The faster these movements, the higher you will jump.

Use your whole body when you jump, not just your legs. You can gain added force by swinging your arms upward and lifting your torso. Try this. Stand with your legs completely straight. Now, swing your arms upward and arch your back. If you do this vigorously enough, your feet will leave the ground. Your arms and torso can add inches to your jump.

FIG 5.10: *jumping to spike*

Make sure that you drive BOTH arms upward when you jump. Lifting only one arm causes your body to twist as you leave the ground. Some hitters raise only their hitting arm when they jump. This rotates their hitting shoulder toward the net, decreasing their power and range. Other hitters raise only their non-hitting arm, turning the non-hitting shoulder further towards the net. Leaving the hitting arm down also creates a long, slow armswing.

Judge the set and adjust your approach so that you can jump almost straight upward, landing only 12-24 inches forward of where you jumped. You will jump your highest by directing all the forces of your jump (your arms, torso, and leg thrust) straight up, vertically. The forward momentum of your approach, then, will carry you slightly forward.

You will often hear others telling hitters to jump straight up. This should not be taken literally. In order to actually jump straight up, your leg thrust would have to oppose your forward momentum, as though you were jumping back. This, of course, would reduce your vertical lift.

Be careful, however, that you DO NOT float forward more than 12-24 inches. 'Broad jumping' can cause you to float past the set, leaving the ball behind your hitting shoulder as you swing. Floating forward can also cause you to go into the net, or land across the center line, especially on tight sets. This is not only a rule violation, but it is dangerous. Most ankle and knee injuries in volleyball are caused by hitters (and blockers) floating into and under the net.

Your jump should leave you in the air, ready to swing. As you leave the ground and your arms rise above head level:
1) pull the elbow of your hitting arm back and slightly away from your body;
2) keep your elbow angle at about 90 degrees;
3) keep your hitting hand forward of your elbow;
4) make sure your hitting hand is open, relaxed, and curved in the shape of the ball.

The Armswing

While your approach and jump are one continuous motion, there should be a definite pause before you swing. At the peak of your jump, just before your body starts to fall, there is a noticeable period of motionlessness; you appear to hang in the air. Time your approach so that you jump and hang . . . then hit the ball (BEFORE your body begins to descend).

Most hitters start their swing by lowering the non-hitting arm. Lowering the non-hitting arm pulls the torso forward, causing a slight piking action. The action of the non-hitting arm and torso drives the hitting shoulder forward and starts the swing of the hitting arm.

When you pull your non-hitting arm down, bend your elbow so that your hand stays close to your torso. Otherwise, your arm could move forward and snag the net. Also, make sure that you pull your arm down in front of your torso, not to the side. Pulling your arm to the side will cause you to twist in the air; your hitting shoulder moves forward, toward the net and past the ball.

Piking your torso delivers added power to the swing. Be careful, however, that you do not pike too much. Piking your chest too far forward lowers your shoulders. Essentially, you make yourself shorter.

The sequence of a typical armswing is as follows:
1) first, your non-hitting arm and trunk;
2) then, your upper arm and hitting elbow;
3) then your forearm and hitting hand;
4) then your wrist-snap.

This sequence builds power that is delivered to the ball at contact. To be effective, an armswing should contain each of the following elements:
1) The hitting hand should accelerate throughout the swing; the greater the hand speed, the more powerful the spike will be.
2) The armswing should be quick and compact, allowing the hitter to wait until the ball nears the point of contact before starting the swing.
3) The swing must contact the ball at the player's highest reach.

You will observe many different armswing used in volleyball. Some generate more power than others, some are quicker, some provide more consistency. Generally, two things differentiate the various armswings:
1) the initial position of the hitting arm and hand, and
2) the path of the hitting hand during the swing.

THE RECOMMENDED ARMSWING   The most distinguishing characteristic of this swing is that your hand remains forward of the elbow when you pull your hitting arm back into position to start the swing. Keeping your hand forward of the elbow allows your upper arm to move farther back, well beyond the shoulder. When you swing, your arm rotates 120-150 degrees around the shoulder joint. You generate power by using the strong shoulder and chest muscles to drive your hitting arm up and forward to the ball (fig 5.11).

As you pull your elbow (and forearm) back, keep your elbow a little higher than shoulder level. Your hitting arm should be bent about 90 degrees at the elbow; this will place your hitting hand just outside your shoulder. If you bring your hand closer to your head, your swing will be much longer and slower. If your arm is too straight, you will lose power.

FIG 5.11: *the recommended armswing*

This swing is similar to a throwing motion of an infielder. Your hitting arm rotates around the shoulder joint, driving your upper arm and elbow (NOT your hand) up and forward, toward the ball. If your arm is relaxed, your forearm and hand should naturally move around behind, to the rear of your elbow. If they do not, your arm may be too tense; relax your arm, especially your wrist and hitting hand. Keep your arm bent at about 90 degrees (at the elbow).

The remaining sequence follows naturally; you will not have to think about it. As your elbow moves forward of your shoulder, your arm straightens. Your forearm whips forward, accelerating your hand up to the ball. At the end of your swing, your hand accelerates, like the end of a whip. Your hand snaps forward (termed the 'wrist snap') as you contact the ball. This action is similar to the snapping of a wet towel.

Keep your hitting hand open and relaxed throughout the approach, jump, and armswing. A relaxed hitting hand is critical to the whip-like wrist snap of your armswing.

The HIGH, SHORT ARMSWING (fig 5.12)   This   armswing   is   fairly common, especially among women volleyball players. It is shorter, and much more compact, than other swings.

The hitter brings their hitting arm straight up when they jump. Then, they pull the hitting hand back behind their head or ear while keeping the elbow high.

The player swings by driving their forearm and hand up and forward to the ball. The arm swings primarily from the elbow (120-150 degrees), with only a moderate amount of shoulder rotation (about 30 degrees).

FIG 5.12: *high, short armswing*

The advantage of the high, short swing is its compactness. The swing is short, so the hitter can wait until the ball is close before swinging. This makes timing the swing much easier. The high initial elbow position also allows hitters to contact the ball consistently at their highest reach. This is especially valuable to hitters lacking in height or jumping ability.

Unfortunately, this swing does not provide as much power as other swings. The swing is made primarily from the elbow. There is not enough shoulder rotation to generate great arm speed. You gain accuracy and consistency at the expense of power.

The LONG, LOOPING ARMSWING (fig 5.13)   This armswing is not commonly used by trained volleyball players, and it is not recommended here. It is a complex technique, one that is difficult to master. The armswing consists of a long, circular motion, similar to the throw of an outfielder.

When the player jumps, the hitting arm rises to about shoulder level. Almost immediately, the player drops the arm back down, well below chest level. The arm continues to loop around behind and back up towards the ball. The path of the hitting hand arm is long and circular.

FIG 5.13: *a long, looping armswing*

The long, circular motion of this armswing can generate considerable power. However, it takes more time to complete the loop and bring the hitting hand back around to the ball. Hitters must start the swing when the ball is still far from the point of contact. The loop is similar to a big hitch in a baseball or swing. It generates power, but it makes timing the swing more difficult. Power is gained at the expense of accuracy and consistency.

Spike Direction

Being able to direct the spike is a major factor in the success of any spiker. Even if you jump high and hit the ball hard, you will have little success when you always hit into the same area.

FIG 5.14a: *hitting straight ahead*

Think of a line from running from your hitting shoulder and going directly through the ball. Your greatest power lies in this line. Measure your approach so that the ball is directly between your shoulder and the area you want to attack. To hit down-the-line, line the ball up directly in front of your hitting shoulder (fig 5.14a). To hit cross-court, keep the ball just inside your hitting shoulder (fig 5.14b). Use the ball-to-shoulder alignment as the foundation for your spike direction. From this foundation, you can still turn the spike.

FIG 5.14b: *hitting cross-court*

Some hitters twist their body in the air, turning the spike by changing the ball-to-shoulder alignment. Hitters can also do this to realign the hitting shoulder when the set is inaccurate. This can be a valuable tool in some situations, but DO NOT make it a habit; turning your body tells the blockers where you're likely to hit.

A more effective way to turn the spike is by turning your wrist-snap (fig 5.15). Your wrist-snap, then, will be in a slightly different direction than your armswing. By turning your wrist, you can change the direction of your spike at the last possible moment. This gives you a deceptive attack and allows you to maneuver the ball around the blockers.

FIG 5.15

Beware of trying to turn the ball too sharply in this manner; cutting the ball radically will cost you power. The decrease in power is proportional to the amount you turn the spike. A slight turn of the wrist results in only slightly less power; a large turn decreases your power significantly. Generally, you can turn the ball about 10-15 degrees without noticeably effecting your spike velocity.

What portion of the balls surface you strike is another factor in spike direction. For example, hitting the left side of the ball will send your spike to the right; hit the right side and your spike goes left. This is sometimes done when hitting off-speed shots, especially in the outdoor, two-person game. It should be noted, however, that this is seldom done when spiking with power . . . not intentionally, anyway!

Contact with the Ball

Typically, the whole hand does not strike the ball all at once. The contact, though nearly simultaneous, is actually a sequence (fig 5.16):
1) first, the lower half of the palm
2) followed immediately by the rest of the palm, and
3) (almost immediately) by the fingers.

FIG 5.16: *contact with the ball*

This sequence delivers the force of your armswing to the ball. The hardness of your hitting hand is an important factor in transferring force to the ball. The harder your hitting hand, the more power you deliver to the ball. If your hand is soft, you absorb some of the ball's rebound; power is lost. Your lower palm area is a relatively hard surface, so you gain power by driving that area into the ball.

Control of the spike is determined by the amount of the ball's surface you contact. If you make your hand small and tight, for instance, you will cover less of the ball and, thus, have less control. If you spread your hand, you will cover more of the ball and, thus, gain more control.

To spike effectively, you need both power and control. If you gain power at the expense of control, you will make far too many hitting errors. If you gain control at the expense of power, your spiking will not be very effective. The ideal hitting hand should provide both.

open hand
FIG 5.17

OPEN HAND (fig 5.17)　　The open hand, which we recommend here, gives you control without sacrificing power. Hold your hand out in front of you. Spread your fingers about one-half inch apart, with the tip of your thumb about an inch from your index finger. DO NOT spread your fingers too much. This makes your hand and fingers weaker, and it stiffens your wrist action.

Curve your hand and fingers in the shape of the ball. This way, your fingers contact the ball just after your lower palm. If your hand is straight, the spike may be gone before your fingers reach the ball. Be careful, also, not to curve your fingers too much. Your fingers, then, might contact the ball before your lower hand does, costing you both power and control.

You want your hitting hand to be somewhat tense and hard. But, you also want it relaxed enough so that your wrist bends freely. Remember, the whip-like action of your wrist-snap depends on your wrist flexing freely.

cupped hand
FIG 5.18

CUPPED HAND (fig 5.18)　　We do NOT recommend that you hit with your hand cupped, though you will find many players who do. It is often taught to younger players in hopes that the hard hitting surface will help the players hit the ball, rather than merely slinging it across the net.

The cupped hand is formed by pressing the fingers and thumb tightly together. This provides a hard hitting surface, but one that is relatively small. Tightly pressing the fingers and thumb stiffens the whole hand, which restricts the wrist-snap.

the fist
FIG 5.19

FIST (fig 5.19)　　We also do NOT recommend hitting the ball with your fist, even though it makes a very hard contact surface. In recreational play, you might see players trying to spike with their fist. It is rare, however, that you will see a trained player using their fist to spike.

Without the fingers wrapping over the ball, the fist provides a very small contact surface, one that provides very little control. You might gain power, but at the expense of control; your spike could go anywhere.

Follow-through and Landing

As you strike the ball, your hitting arm should be totally straight. Your armswing and wrist snap will naturally cause your arm to bend at the elbow after you contact the ball. Bring your hitting hand back toward your body as your arm follows through. Otherwise, your hand will continue forward, toward the net. On close sets (those within about 18 inches) this could cause your follow-through to touch the net, which, of course, is illegal. A straight arm follow-through will also cause you to be more out of balance as you land.

As you return to the floor, use your leg muscles to absorb the momentum of your body's descent and gain your balance (fig 5.20).

FIG 5.20: *follow-through and landing*

Spiking the ball does not always end the play. If you are blocked, or if your opponent's dig sends the ball back across the net, prepare to pass or spike again. If the opposing team controls the dig, move to your blocking position and prepare to play defense. No matter how well you hit the spike, do not celebrate while the ball is still in play.

The Tip Shot (dink)

The tip shot is a change-of-pace variation of the spike. The 'open hand tip' is the variation more commonly used in 6-person play. It is more deceptive, and more accurate than the other version.

The 'cut shot' variation is more commonly used in 2- and 3-person outdoor play, where the open hand tip is generally illegal. It is also used occasionally as a change-of-pace shot in the indoor game. If the open hand tip is ever outlawed in the indoor game, as is often discussed, the cut shot would be a valuable addition to a player's repertoire.

For either tip to be effective, you must jump and swing exactly as you would if you were hitting your most powerful spike. Change only the end of your armswing, just before you contact the ball.

The Open Hand Tip (fig 5.21)

FIG 5.21: *tipping the ball*

During the last 6 inches of your swing, slow your hand and spread your fingers. Contact the ball with your index, middle, and ring finger (down to the 1st or 2nd knuckle). Slight contact may be made with the thumb and little finger, but it is not necessary. Guide the ball up and over the block. Remember, you want your shot to fall in front of the backcourt diggers, so do not tip the ball too hard.

94

You'll see many hitters who jump and immediately extend their hitting arm straight up. Some even shape their hand for the tip before they jump. When you change your armswing, you telegraph the tip. Your opponents will have little trouble getting to the ball, passing it to their setter, and spiking it back at you.

When you make an open hand tip, your wrist does not have to be locked. However, very little, if any, wrist action is needed. Any wrist action you use must be in the same direction as your armswing. DO NOT use wrist action to change the direction of the tip; this is illegal.

The Cut Shot

The cut shot is somewhat similar to the open hand tip.
1) the swing should look exactly like a full arm swing;
2) slow the hitting hand just before contact, no sooner;
3) DO NOT telegraph the shot before contact.

The differences in the cut shot occur just before you strike the ball. One difference is your hand's contact surface. When using the cut shot, you contact the ball with the lower palm area of the hitting hand (fig 5.22). Often, the fingers do not even contact the ball, though sometimes they do.

The hand does not strike the ball solidly, it is more like a glancing blow. The hand rolls over the ball as the heel of the palm makes contact. The action is similar to what you might do with a table tennis paddle.

FIG 5.22: *the cut shot*

Unlike the open hand tip, you use wrist action to make the cut shot. Your wrist snaps the hand over (or around) the ball, hitting it with a glancing shot. Your wrist action also directs the shot. Because the contact is mostly a rebound, using wrist action in the shot is perfectly legal.

Hitting Quick Sets

Some think that hitting a quick set is an advanced skill . . . and if your team passes poorly, it certainly is! But, poor passing is what makes this skill difficult. If you pass accurately, hitting a quick attack is no more difficult than other tempo plays. Quick attacks, even in recreational play, have become quite common.

Tempo attacks, in general, require you to time the flight of the pass rather than the set. The actual timing depends on many factors (e.g., your quickness, which approach you use, trajectory of the pass, etc.). Generally, tempo attacks require you to start your approach before the setter sets the ball. For example, when hitting a 2nd-tempo attack, you might start your approach when the pass is about 3-5 feet from the setter's hands.

TIMING   When you hit a 1st-tempo (quick) attack, start your approach according to when the passer contacts the ball (fig 5.23):
1)   QUICK APPROACH - when the passer contacts the ball,
2)   3- or 4-STEP APPROACH - just before the passer contacts the ball.

FIG 5.23: _as the ball is passed_

Turn your head and watch the ball being as it is being passed. Stay focused on the flight of the pass. You do not need to look for the setter; he or she will be going to the ball. As the pass nears the net, you will see the setter in your peripheral vision. When you see both the pass and the setter, NOT before, focus your attention on the setter.

Adjust your speed of your approach according to the pass trajectory. Speed up or slow down according to the flight of the ball:

1)   LOW trajectory pass - speed up
2)   HIGH trajectory pass - slow down.

FIG 5.24: *as the pass nears the setter*

One of the most important elements in hitting quick sets is to be in the air BEFORE the ball is set (fig 5.25). Then, you have more time to swing, and to see the block. You will be able to hit with power and accuracy. In addition, your setter (who is looking up at the pass) can see you better when you are in the air. If you are still on the ground, the setter can only guess where you are.

FIG 5.25: *as the ball is set*

Many hitters struggle with quick attacks because they jump as, or after, the setter delivers the ball. They have to rush their armswing just to make contact, losing both power and control. Sometimes, the ball passes through the hitting zone before the hitter even has a chance to swing.

LOCATION   Quick sets are usually placed 2-3 feet off the net. This gives the hitter plenty of room to swing. You, as a hitter, should measure your approach accordingly, so that you jump 3-4 feet from the net. Jumping too close to the net makes the attack difficult to hit, and easy to block.

Make your approach so that you jump within 2-3 feet of the setter (fig 5.26a). DO NOT just run to the middle: the set takes longer getting to you, and you wind up hitting right in front of the opposing blocker. When you jump next to your setter, however, the attack is quicker and much more effective.

(a)   (b)

(a) pass close to the net   FIG 4.26   *pass away from the net (b)*

When the pass is away from the net (4-8 feet), you will need to stay a little further away from the setter, 3-5 feet (fig 4.26b). Leave your setter room to put the ball in front of your shoulder. If you are too close, the set comes from right behind your armpit . . . a difficult ball to hit.

When hitting quick sets, use a short, fast armswing (such as the recommended armswing, page 87). Avoid using a long, looping armswing. If you loop your swing, the set may pass though your hitting zone before your hand can get there.

Key Points

THE APPROACH
1. Use your approach to move to the set.
    a. Move to the set and jump so that the ball is above and just in front of your hitting shoulder when you swing.
    b. Adjust your approach according to the set. For example,
        1) if the set is away from the net, shorten the length of your strides;
        2) if the ball is set inside or close to the net, lengthen your strides.
        3) DO NOT change the number of steps you take;
        4) DO NOT change the sequence of the steps.
2. Basic approach patterns
    a. Quick 3-step approach: primarily used to hit 1st-tempo sets.
        1) Right handers - short left, right and left.
        2) Left handers - short right, left and right.
    b. Basic 3-step approach: a fast, but short approach
        1) Right handers - strong left, right and left.
        2) Left handers - strong right, left and right.
    c. 4-step approach: the most versatile approach, the most commonly recommended
        1) Right handers - short right, strong left, right and left.
        2) Left handers - short left, strong right, left and right.
3. Transition phase
    a. The last two steps are a distinctive one . . . two sequence.
        1) Right handers - right, then left.
        2) Left handers - left, then right.
    b. DO NOT hop onto both feet.
4. Prepare for the jump during the transition phase:
    a. Bend your knees to 90-110 degrees;
    b. pull both arms back behind you;
    c. lower your torso slightly;
    d. keep your head up and your eyes on the ball.
5. COMMON ERRORS
    a. aligning the ball behind the hitting shoulder, or directly over the head;
    b. adding (or dropping) steps during the approach;
    c. 'goofy-foot' approach;
    d. pulling the arms back too late, or too soon.

THE JUMP
1. Start to jump as soon as your last step touches down.
    a. Swing your arms forward and upward;
    b. lift your torso, leaving your back slightly arched in the air;

    c.   forcefully push downward with your legs;

2.   As you leave the ground, prepare for your swing:
    a.   Pull your ELBOW directly back, leaving the hitting hand forward;
    b.   DO NOT pull the hand back first.
    c.   Your hitting hand should remain open and relaxed.

3.   COMMON ERRORS
    a.   stopping . . . then jumping;
    b.   lifting only one arm during the jump;
    c.   dropping the hitting arm to waist level as you leave the ground.

THE ARMSWING

1.   Start your swing with the following sequence:
    a.   lower your non-hitting arm,
    b.   pike your torso slightly forward.

2.   Drive your hitting elbow and upper arm up and forward, toward the ball.
    a.   Drive the elbow, NOT the hand, toward the ball;
    b.   as the elbow comes forward, the forearm and hitting hand will naturally move to the rear of the elbow.

3.   Immediately, without letting the hitting hand come to a stop,
    a.   drive your hitting hand up and forward to meet the ball.
    b.   at the end of the swing, snap your hand over the top of the ball.

4.   COMMON ERRORS
    a.   keeping the non-hitting arm up, or dropping it as the hitting arm swings (using a swimming type action);
    b.   hitting with a stiff wrist.

CONTACT WITH THE BALL

1.   At contact, your hand should be open and relaxed.
    a.   Your fingers should be spread comfortably;
    b.   they should be curved in the shape of the ball.

2.   COMMON ERRORS
    a.   making the hitting hand and fingers stiff;
    b.   cupping the hitting hand.

FOLLOW-THROUGH

1.   Gain your balance as you land.
2.   Prepare to make your next play.

THE TIP
1. Your armswing should look exactly like your most powerful swing.
2. Slow your swing just before you contact the ball.
3. OPEN HAND TIP
    a. contact the ball primarily with the middle three fingers;
    b. use very little wrist action.
4. CUT SHOT
    a. contact the ball with the lower palm area;
    b. use wrist action to roll your hand over the ball and direct the shot.
5. Tip the ball softly, so that it falls in front of hte defensive players.
6. COMMON ERRORS
    a. immediately extending the hitting arm as you jump (telegraphing the shot);
    b. using too much wrist action (open hand tip), or too little (cut shot);
    c. tipping the ball straight, or down, instead of up over the block.

THE QUICK ATTACK
1. Time the pass, not the set:
    a. take your 1st step about when the passer contacts the ball;
    b. speed up if the pass is low, slow down if the pass is high.
2. Go to the setter, not the center of the net.
3. Jump 3-4 feet from the net, so that you contact the ball 2-3 feet from the net.
4. COMMON ERRORS
    a. watching the setter, instead of the passer and the pass;
    b. jumping as, or after, the ball is set;
    c. going to the center area instead of to the setter.

OFFENSIVE DESIGN

Offensive strategies coordinate the individual skills of passing, setting, and spiking to attack an opponent's defense. Offensive systems are often designed to maximize a team's own abilities, or to attack an opponent's weaknesses. It is important to note that any strategy is only as effective as the execution of the individual skills involved. If you use a system that is more advanced than your skill development, that system could hurt you more than it helps you.

Offensive strategies generally define how a team intends to attack their opponent. This includes:
1) how the team will receive the serve (the formation);
2) designation of the setter;
3) deployment of the hitters;
4) location and tempo of the attack options.

Basic Serve Receive Formations

A team's serve receive formation specifies each player's starting position for that particular rotation. Receive formations vary somewhat from team to team, amd even from rotation to rotation. There are, however, several basic formations commmonly used. These are generally identified by the number of players used to receive the serve. Recreational teams often use five players to cover the court; competitive teams may use as few as two or three passers.

Teams often modify these basic formations to suit their personnel, or to enhance their attack options. If you understand the basic formations, however, you can easily adapt to the variations you might encounter as you continue on in the sport.

5-PERSON RECEIVE The 5-person formation (fig 6.1a) lets each passer cover a small area of the court. The passers, then, can reach the ball easily, which allows them to pass with good alignment most of the time.

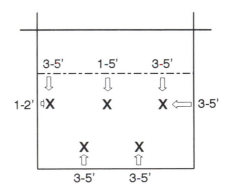

5-person receive: FIG 6.1a

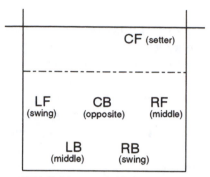

FIG 6.1b: *typical formation*

The 5-person receive is rarely used in competition. Because the passing formation includes every player except the setter (fig 6.1b), the team's weakest passers are always exposed. The opposing server, of course, aims at these passers. The worst passers, then, wind up passing most of the serves, while the team's best passers seldom touch the ball.

4-PERSON RECEIVE   The 4-person formation (fig 6.2) is fairly common in both recreation and competition. It removes the middle person from the pattern all together. To cover the void, the right side passers start closer to the middle. Since serves crossing to their sideline are in the air longer, they can still reach balls served near the sideline area.

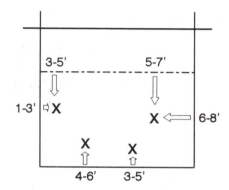

4-person receive: FIG 6.2a

The players nearest the 3-meter line (usually the two outside hitters) should pass every short serve. If the hitters fail to cover the short middle area, the deep receivers must either charge forward, or start closer to the net. This makes it difficult for them to handle deep serves. The team's passing will be weak in the deep areas, as well in the short middle. The key to success in the 4-person receive is the passing of the two hitters.

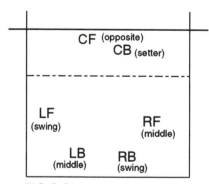

FIG 6.2b: *typical formation*

The 4-person formation, of course, does not require every player to pass. Usually, a team moves one of the hitters to the net (fig 6.2a). Since this hitter does not pass, he or she is often designated to hit quick sets.

104

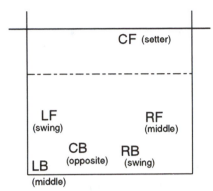

FIG 6.2c: *typical formation*

Sometimes teams move a back row player (usually the weakest passer) to the endline (fig 6.2b), removing the player from the passing formation. Most often, this occurs when the setter is in the front row.

3-PERSON RECEIVE The 3-person receive (fig 6.3a) has become a very popular formation. However, it may not be well suited for all teams. It requires fairly advanced skills, athletic ability, and playing experience. Passers who lack these qualities could struggle in the 3-person formation.

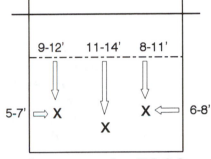

3-person receive: FIG 6.3a

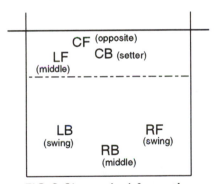

FIG 6.3b: *typical formation*

The 3-person provides a lot of flexibility in positioning the hitters and passers. Often, the team's best passers (usually the swing hitters) occupy two of the three passing spots. This allows the best passers to cover more of the court, and handle more serves. Of course, each passer must cover a larger area; thus, the need for outstanding abilities.

The exact positioning of players in each of these formations depends on the playing system used, and the specific abilities of the team's personnel. The illustrations provided are only basic examples. Each of these receiving patterns has as many variations as coaches have imagination.

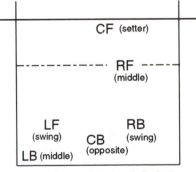

typical formation: FIG 6.3c

Basic Offensive Systems

Teams often designate players by the primary function they serve (fig 6.4a and 6.4b, below). An offense specifies which players are to pass, which players are available to spike, and which player is to set. Common designations are:
1) setters;
2) opposite;
3) middle hitter/blockers;
4) swing-hitters.

A team may employ one or more setters in their overall design. But, only one player is designated to set for any given rotation. This player is responsible for delivering the set regardless of the pass. Unless the designated setter cannot possibly reach the ball, no other player should step in and set.

Teams that use two setters generally place these players opposite each other in the lineup. Then, one setter is always in the back row while the other is in front row. For example, if one setter starts in the right back, the other starts in the left front. When one rotates to the front row, the other rotates to the back row.

Teams that use only one setter designate another hitter to play opposite the setter. The 'opposite' is usually a team's strongest hitter. Often, they are called on to hit from the the back row when the setter is at the net.

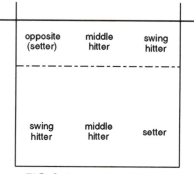

FIG 6.4a: *typical lineup*

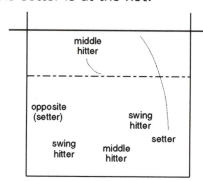

typical formation: FIG 6.4b

Most teams designate two specific players to play the middle hitter/blocker position. Because middle hitters hit in the middle and block all along the net, they are often among your tallest players. Usually, middle hitters are positioned opposite each other in the lineup. Then, one is always at the net.

The designation for the two remaining hitters varies a great deal from team to team. One common term is left-side hitter, since they often block and hit on the left side. Swing-hitter is also a popular term. Swing-hitters are usually the team's best passers. Both should always be present in the passing formation.

THE 4-2 SYSTEM   The 4-2 is a basic offensive system that employs two setters. Whichever setter is in the front row is the designated setter. The other two front row players are used as spikers. This system is termed a 4-2 because it employs four hitters and two setters.

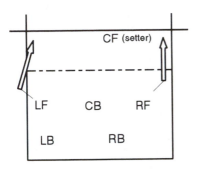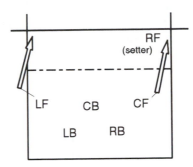

FIG 6.5: *with the hitters outside*

Some teams place their hitters near the sideline where they can easily spike from the outside attack areas (fig 6.5). These hitters can also move in from the outside and hit in the middle area. More often, though, teams attack the middle by starting one of the hitters near the center of the court (fig 6.6).

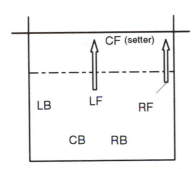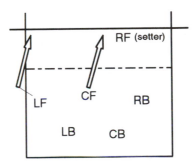

with a middle hitter: FIG 6.6

The advantage of the 4-2 is its simplicity. The setter is always near the net, and the hitters can always be positioned near the outside. This can be advantageous for teams that pass poorly. When the pass is inaccurate, it is especially difficult to set and hit the middle attack.

However, the 4-2 limits a team's options by having only two front row hitters available. The offense is predictable, allowing the opposing defense to place two or three blockers against every attack.

THE 6-2 SYSTEM   A team can overcome the limitations of having only two hitters by designating a back row player to be the setter. Then, all three front row players are available to spike. This system is generally termed a 6-2 because it employs two setters and all six players hit.

The 6-2 has a number of shortcomings, especially if the passing is inconsistent. When the pass is not accurate, it is difficult to set the ball to the middle hitter. The ball can only be set to the outside. The middle hitter (usually a big spiker), is then useless.

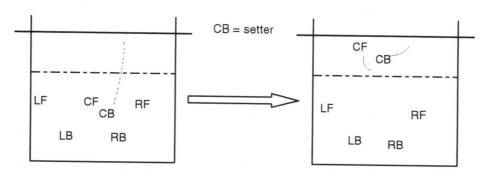

FIG 6.7a: *moving the setter closer to the net*

Another problem with the 6-2 is that the setter is moving to the net from the back row. Too often, they are not near the net (or are still moving) as the ball is passed. This takes them out of position, and slows their movement to the pass. Teams often modify their passing formations so that the setter can start nearer the net (fig 6.7a and 6.7b).

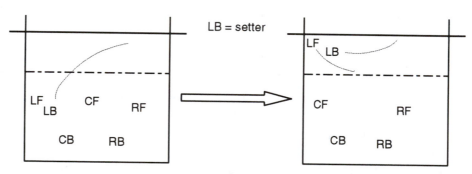

moving the setter closer to the net: FIG 6.7b

Perhaps the biggest disadvantage of the 6-2 offense is that teams rarely have two setters who are both very good hitters, AND have similar setting skills. If the setters are too different, it can throw off the hitters' timing and rhythm.

THE 5-1 SYSTEM   The 5-1 avoids this problem by using only one setter. The prevailing thought is that an offense functions best when the best setter sets every ball. The hitters, then, always get the best possible set. And, they only have to learn one setter's delivery and characteristics. The 5-1 is currently the most popular offensive system.

The 5-1 is a combination of the systems discussed on the previous pages. When the setter is in the back row, it has the characteristics of a 6-2 system. When the setter is in the front row, it is similar to the 4-2.

The disadvantage of the 5-1 occurs when the setter is in the front row, roughly half the time. Having only two front row hitters limits the attack options, just as it does with the 4-2. Teams using the 5-1 generally compensate by moving their hitters around, varying their attack locations. At higher levels, teams also use back row hitters to compensate.

Offensive Strategies

Volleyball teams run plays to create an attack advantage. Often, plays are designed to create one-on-one hitting situations, one hitter against only one blocker. Plays may also try to isolate strong hitters against weaker blockers.

Some teams call plays individually for their hitters. Each hitter, for example, calls out what set they want to hit. Other teams run their plays in combinations. For example, one hitter is in the air for a 1st-tempo set, while another hitter moves in for a 2nd-tempo attack.

Each play communicates the attack location and tempo, for both the setter and the hitters. Unfortunately, play terminology varies from place to place, from team to team, and even from player to player. What some would call a 'four', others call a 'five'; what some call a 'five', others call a 'D', etc.

The following, we believe, is a good system of terminology. Obviously, this is not the only system. But it is very descriptive, and its usage is fairly common.

LOCATION   Start by dividing the net into nine equal areas (fig 6.8a), each a little more than 3 feet wide. The zone next to the left sideline is attack area 1. As you move along the net left-to-right, the next area is zone 2, then zone 3, etc. Zone 5 is in the center; zone 9 is next to the right sideline.

Each zone is an attack area. Zone 1, for example, is the left outside attack area. Typically, passes are directed to the setter between zones 5 and 7.

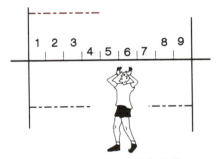

pass on target: FIG 6.8a

Some attack locations are defined relative to the position of the setter. For example, 1st-tempo attacks often are hit directly in front of the setter, no matter where the pass goes. To allow for this, the middle zones are numbered relative to the setter, no matter where the setter receives the pass. Zone 5 becomes the zone directly in front of the setter; zone 4 is one zone beyond zone 5. Zone 6 becomes the zone directly behind the setter; zone 7 is always one zone beyond zone 6. These zones float with the setter as the setter moves along the net to receive the pass (fig 6.8b and 6.8c).

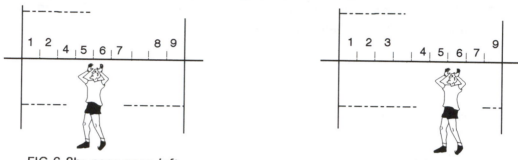

FIG 6.8b: *pass goes left*   *pass goes right:* FIG 6.8c

ATTACK TEMPO   Tempo is the speed at which the attack occurs. It is a function of the peak height of the set. Usually, a hitter times the set. When hitting fast-tempo attacks, however, the hitter times the pass, instead.

A 1st-tempo (quick) is a very fast attack. Generally, the hitter starts when the ball is passed, and jumps before the ball is set. The ball should be set as high as the hitter can reach. For tall hitters, this may be two feet or more above the net; for shorter hitters, it may be less than one foot above the net. In any case, the hitter should hit the set as (or just before) the ball peaks.

A 2nd-tempo set is slower, but it is still a fairly fast attack. The hitter starts when the pass is in flight, the ball on its way to the setter. He or she is usually one step away from jumping when the setter delivers the set. The set peaks 4-6 feet above the net, depending on the spiker's hitting height. The play is designed so that the set peaks and falls before the hitter hits the ball.

A 3rd-tempo is a higher set (peaking 5-8 feet above the net), one that creates a fairly slow attack. In many systems, the 3rd-tempo is used for the basic set. In other systems, it is not used at all.

The basic set (sometimes termed a '0') is a high set, peaking 7-10 feet above the net. In most cases, the hitter starts their approach about the time the setter releases the ball.

110

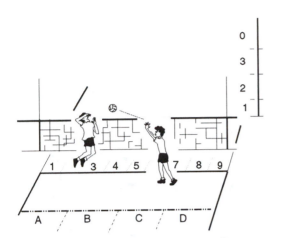

31 is a 1st-tempo attack in zone 3
FIG 6.9

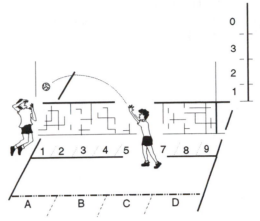

12 is a 2nd-tempo attack in zone 1
FIG 6.10

PLAY-SET DESIGNATION   The system presented here defines plays by both location and tempo. The attack is designated by a double digit number. The first digit is the location, the second digit is the tempo. For example:

		PLAY	LOCATION	TEMPO
1)	fig 6.9	31	zone 3	1st tempo
2)	fig 6.10	12	zone 1	2nd-tempo
3)	fig 6.11	72	zone 7	2nd-tempo
4)	fig 6.12	90	zone 9	basic high set

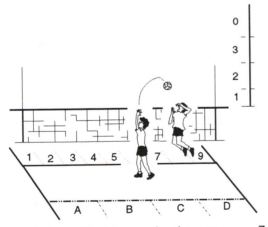

72 is a 2nd-tempo backset to zone 7
FIG 6.11

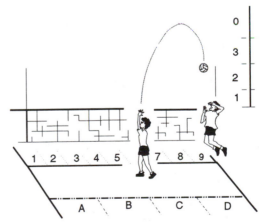

90 is a high backset to zone 9
FIG 6.12

111

It is becomming increasingly common for teams at all levels to have backrow players spiking from the backcourt, setting the ball near, or just inside of the 3-meter line (fig 6.13). Backrow players may spike so long as they jump from behind the 3-meter line.

Teams that use backrow hitters classify their backrow attack areas. Zones 'A' and 'D' are near the left and right sidelines, respectively. Zones 'B' and 'C' are to the left and right of center. The middle area is known as the 'pipe'.

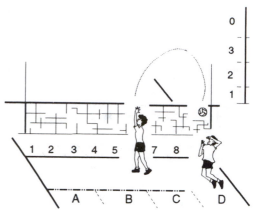

backrow attack in zone D
FIG 6.13

PLAY-SET DESIGN   An offense will usually have many plays. Generally, the more advanced the team, the more plays they will have have available. Note in the examples that follow: each play combination includes and outlet, a hitter who is ready to hit a high set in the event of a bad pass.

Some plays are designed to isolate one hitter against a single blocker. The set is low enough so that the middle blocker does not have time to move and join the block. Examples of isolation plays are the (12) set to the LF in figure 6.14a, and the (92) set to the RF in figure 6.14b.

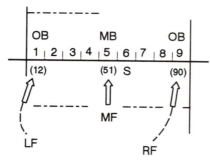

FIG 6.14a: *front 'shoot' set*

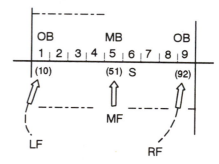

back 'shoot' set: FIG 6.14b

Other types of plays involve combinations of hitters coordinated to attack the total block. Generally, combination plays fall into one of three catagories:
1)   plays that spread the blockers;
2)   crossing patterns;
3)   plays that influence blockers away from the attack location;
4)   hitter-option plays, where the hitter calls the attack location.

Spread plays use the quick attack to make the opposing middle blocker move away from the center. The ball is then set in the opposite direction. The speed of the play combines with the separation to prevent the middle blocker from recovering and reaching the second hitter. Examples of such plays are provided in figures 6.15a and 6.15b.

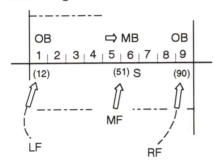

quick 'one', with a front 'lob'
FIG 6.15a

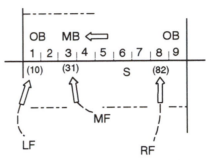

quick '31', with a back 'two'
FIG 6.15b

Crossing patterns move the second hitter across the path of the quick hitter (fig 6.16a and 6.16b). This makes the blockers job more difficult:

1)   the outside blocker follows the hitter by looping around the middle blocker;
2)   the blockers switch assignments;
3)   the team 'stacks' their blockers, a complex blocking scheme developed to counter crossing patterns ('stack blocking', discussed in chapter 11).

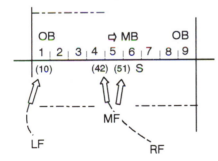

FIG 6.16a: *basic 'X' play*

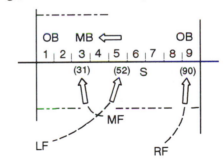

'31-X' play: FIG 6.16b

Influence plays use the repeated success of a base play to influence blockers away from the actual attack. When a team scores on an 'X' play a number of times, the 'fake-X' can be effective (fig 6.17a, next page). When a team runs the quick middle well, the 'quick-slide' can be effective (fig 6.17b, next page). Keep in mind that influence plays always originate in another play. If you cannot run the base play, the influence play will be ineffective.

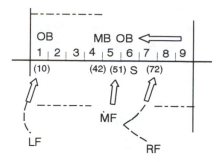

FIG 6.17a: *the fake 'X'*

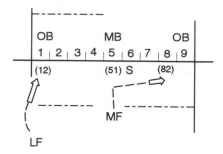

the 'quick-slide': FIG 6.17b

Often, the plays are called before the ball is served. In more advanced systems, however, spikers call out attack options as the play develops. During the spike approach, while the pass is in flight to the setter, the hitter observes the movement of the blockers. The hitter then calls out, and moves to, the attack option that is poorly defended.

In the above example (fig 6.17a), the RF hitter takes an approach path to hit an 'X'. Reading the blockers reaction, RF can either continue on and hit the 'X' (52), or turn and hit the 'fake-X' option (72). In the same way, MF in figure 6.17b reads the blockers and either hits the quick 51 set, or options to the 'quick-slide', depending on the blockers' reactions.

The backrow attack is becoming common in all levels of volleyball play. Some teams use the backrow attacker only in an emergency, when the pass is very bad. Other teams use the backrow attack primarily when their setter is in the front row, to supplement the offense. Some teams, however, use the backrow attacker as an integral part of their offensive strategy. Figures 6.18a and 6.18b are examples of ways in which the back row attack can be utilized.

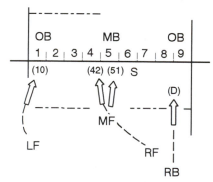

FIG 6.18a: *backrow attack, 'D'*

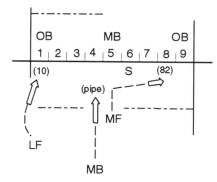

backrow attack, 'pipe': FIG 6.18b

114

DEFENSIVE PHILOSOPHY

Just as the purpose of an offense is to produce an effective attack, the defense is designed to prevent an attack from being successful. A team generally has two lines of defense: the block, and the backcourt diggers. These can either obstruct the opponent's attack (by blocking), or control the attack (by digging) and create a counter-attack of their own.

In addition to blocking and digging, serving also plays a key role in defensive success. It is a role that is often misunderstood.

Serving

The serve can do much more than merely put the ball in play. When the server just puts the ball in play, the other team has an easy time passing the ball. Usually, the pass goes right to the setter, allowing the offense to use all of its attack options. The advantage goes to the offense.

If, however, the serve is difficult to pass, the team's passing breaks down. Then, the offensive options are limited. The offense becomes predictable and the advantage shifts to the defense.

The serve should be seen as a weapon used to attacks the other team's passing. An effective serve, then, is one that is difficult to pass.

Many people emphasize never missing a serve. Serving into the court is certainly important, but it should not be the sole emphasis. Serving effectively, breaking down an opponent's passing, is equally important. The defense gains little by merely lobbing the ball over the net, even if they never miss. Of course, they gain nothing by serving the ball out of bounds, or into the net, either.

A good serve will be effective in each of three areas. It will be accurate, hit with power, and contain some form of ball movement. If a serve is deficient in any of these areas, it will be less productive.

ACCURACY   Accuracy DOES NOT mean never missing a serve, and it seldom means hitting the sidelines. Accuracy means being able to serve the ball to specific areas, attacking an opponent's weakness. For example:
1)   serving at the weakest passer;
2)   serving to weak areas in the opponent's receive formation,
3)   serving the hitters in areas that make their attack more difficult.

POWER   Fast moving serves are more difficult to pass than ones that move slowly. The speed of the serve gives the passers less time to judge the flight of the ball, make decisions, and move into good passing position. As a result, their passing is less accurate, and more inconsistent.

A major consideration concerning power is the trajectory of the serve. The harder you hit the ball, the flatter the trajectory must be. Most powerful serves only clear the net by 1-3 feet, passing between the net and the tops of the antennae (fig 7.1a). If the serve is higher than this, it is more likely to go out of bounds (fig 7.1b); if it is lower, the ball is more likely to contact the net (fig 7.1c). Remember, serving power and control must be equally matched.

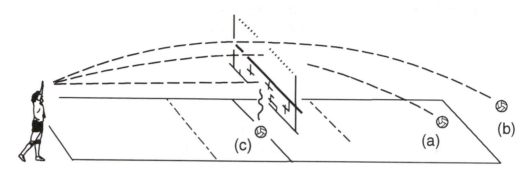

FIG 7.1: *power/trajectory relationship*

MOVEMENT   Movement on the serve can cause the passer to be in poor passing position. Spin serves move in an arc, similar to a curve ball in baseball. This can be effective when the serve is hit with power. The velocity of ball does not give passers much time to judge the ball's arc and move into good passing position. The jump serve is an example of a spin serve that is effective when used by players who can hit it consistently, and with power.

Floater serves move in an unpredictable pattern, similar to a knuckleball in baseball. Consequently, they are difficult to pass. The ball floats as it nears the passer, leaving the player little time to respond. Often, the passer winds up adjusting to the movement by reaching for the ball, causing an errant pass.

Blocking

Blocking is central to defensive play. Most teams try to join two (or three) of their blockers to defend against the spike. Having more blockers, of course, increases the chances of blocking the attack. It also increase the chances of digging the spike, since the court areas left unblocked are smaller.

Most often, the block is positioned to take away the large area in the middle of the court (see fig 7.7, pg 120). By blocking the middle area, a narrow hitting lane on either side of the blockers is left open. The narrow lane is then defended by a backcourt digger. This is usually more effective than blocking one side of the court, and leaving a larger area to be covered by the diggers.

116

INITIAL POSITION   When the other team is receiving the ball (whether by serve, spike, or volley), the front row players become blockers. Immediately, as the ball is crossing the net, the blockers should move to their initial positions. They should be in position before the opponent's pass the ball.

Blockers usually play specific blocking position, regardless of where they were when the play started. For example:
1)   setters/opposite block on the right;
2)   middle hitter\blockers start in the center;
3)   swing-hitters block on the left.

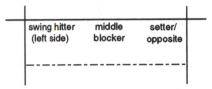

typical initial positions: FIG 7.2

Since offenses usually operate from the right of center, most teams find it advantageous to have their setter block on the right side. When they dig a ball, then, they are in position to set the offensive transition. Teams generally position their best blocker in the middle where they can block all along the net. Swing-hitters, then, block on the left side (fig 7.2).

Advanced level teams sometimes move their blockers around, trying to match up their best blockers against their opponent's strongest attacks. It should be noted that these teams generally have players whose height, athletic ability, experience, and training allow them to play any of the positions. Even in high level competition, however, moving blockers around is uncharacteristic.

Middle blockers have two responsibilities. They are the primary defense against middle attacks. In addition, they must join with the outside blockers to oppose other attacks. To do this, they need to start near the middle.

Outside blockers are primarily responsible for blocking attacks near the sidelines. Their initial position is at the net and, generally, about 3-4 feet in from the sideline (fig 7.3a). Some defenses, however, use the outside blockers to help defend against middle attacks. When this is the case, the outside blockers start closer to the middle, about 6-8 feet from the sideline (fig 7.3b).

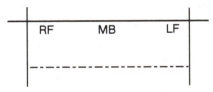

FIG 7.3a: *blockers spread*

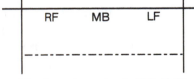

blockers bunched: FIG 7.3b

OUTSIDE BLOCKERS   The positioning of the block is the responsibility of the outside blocker. The block should be positioned in concert with the coverage of the backcourt players. The block seals off a specified area; the backcourt diggers cover the areas left unblocked. When the block is misaligned, the blockers block the same areas covered by the backcourt players. This leaves other areas of the court unguarded, weakening the team's defensive effort.

When the opponent sets the ball to the sideline attack area, the outside blocker away from the attack (the 'off-blocker') should immediately join the backcourt coverage. They must move quickly, away from the net to a digging position. The exact digging position will vary depending on the team's defensive design, but it is generally near the 3-meter line, or beyond (fig 7.4).

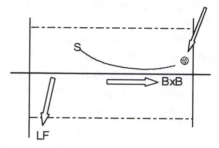

the 'off-side blocker': FIG 7.4

Fast-tempo sets in the middle do not usually give the outside blockers enough time to move to a digging position very far away from the net. The outside blockers reaction to the fast (1st or 2nd-tempo) middle set should be toward the attack. Some defensive systems want the outside blocker (one or both) to join the block (fig 7.5a). Others want the outside blocker to move inside and cover tips (fig 7.5b). Few, if any, defenses want the outside blockers to remain near the sideline.

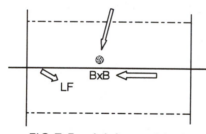

FIG 7.5a: *joining to block*

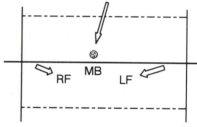

covering the tip: FIG 7.5b

MIDDLE BLOCKERS   The middle blocker's primary responsibility is to block. They block all along the net, against every attack. Generally, teams play their tallest and best blockers in this position. While the middle blocker needs to be tall, they must also be agile enough to move quickly and block outside.

The quick set is usually the first attack that the middle blocker defends. Depending on the blocking strategy employed, the quick attack may or may not be the middle blocker's primary responsibility. Often, joining the outside blocker to oppose the outside attack is a higher priority. Ideally, the middle blocker will be able to defend attacks in the middle as well as those near the sideline areas.

Occasionally, the middle blocker is not able to reach the outside attack in time to block. When this occurs, the player should continue on to the outside to cover short tips and balls deflected off of the outside blocker's hands.

Backcourt Defense

Backcourt defenders, like blockers, should move to their 'ready defensive position' as the ball is sent across the net (by serving, spiking, or volleying). Players should be in their ready position before the other team passes the ball. This position is defined by the team's defensive system (fig 7.6a and 7.6b). In the ready position, players should be prepared to dig quick attacks, passes coming back across the net, and balls the opposing setter dumps over the net.

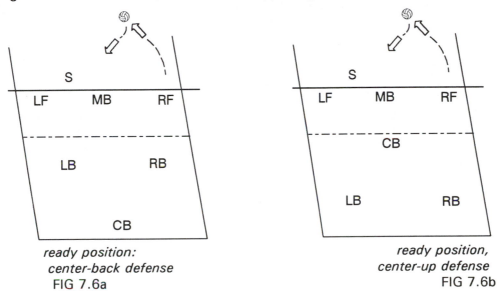

ready position:
center-back defense
FIG 7.6a

ready position,
center-up defense
FIG 7.6b

Once the ball is set, each player should move quickly to their defensive digging position. The team's defensive system determines each player's specific defensive responsibilities, and court positioning. Backcourt players should arrive at their digging positions well before the hitter jumps. This will give them time to make minor adjustments as the hitter jumps, and time to stop and gain their balance before the hitter swings.

The coverage of the backcourt defenders should be coordinated with that of the blockers. Backcourt players are responsible for covering those areas left unguarded by the block. The digging positions, therefore, are in the areas where shots avoiding the block are likely to go. For example (fig 7.7, next page):
1) digging down-the-line (a): near the sideline, 18-23 feet from the net;
2) cross-court spikes (b): near the opposite sideline, 15-20 feet from the net;
3) covering tips (c): near the attack, around the 3-meter line;
4) covering behind the block (d): near the middle, 25-30 feet from the net.

Since the backcourt players are responsible for areas (attacks) left unguarded by the block, the final digging positions are usually determined by the location of the hitter relative to the position of the blockers (known as the hitter-blocker configuration).

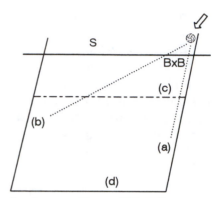

digging positions: FIG 7.7

Players digging down-the-line (a) and cross-court (b) spikes should be in a direct line with the hitter; the blocker should NOT be between the hitter and the digger. Players covering tips (c) and balls over the block (d) would be behind the block (fig 7.7).

Movement to the final digging position should occur before the hitter jumps. The diggers need to be balanced and stable as the hitter begins their swing. The defensive player who is still moving when the ball is hit will not make many plays, and control very few of the digs they do make.

Transition

Defensive play involves more than digging the ball and keeping it in play. A defense that retrieves the ball and merely sends it back across the net does not score many points. To score, the defense must convert digs into offensive opportunities. For the defense to make the transition to offense,

1) the ball must be dug into an area where it can be set;
2) someone with setting ability should be positioned near that area;
3) the blockers must get into position to spike.

The chapter covering individual defense will discuss in detail how to control the dig and pass it to an area. The team's defensive strategy determines the position of the players, and designates who is responsible for setting in transition. Keep in mind, though, that the first priority of every defensive player is to dig the ball. Until the dig is achieved, there are no setters, there are no hitters.

SERVING

An effective serve is one that is difficult to pass. To be effective, the server must have accuracy. Keep in mind that accuracy means more than just hitting the ball into the court; accuracy means serving the ball to an opponent's weakest passers, or to weak areas in their formation. Movement on the ball is another element that makes a serve difficult to pass.

The floater serve is delivered so that the ball in flight has no spin. The airflow around the ball causes the ball to 'float', similar to a knuckleball.

Unlike the floater serve, the spin serve travels in a predictable arc, which is why it is generally less effective. To be productive, spin serves need to be delivered with great velocity. A jump serve is an example of an effective spin serve, though it is a difficult serve to master.

The overhand floater serve most common serve in volleyball, at all levels of play. It is easily learned and quickly mastered. As players gain skill with the technique, they can deliver the floater with both accuracy and velocity. The 'floater' is the serve recommended here (fig 8.1).

FIG 8.1: *serving the ball*

Initial Posture

Start with your hips facing about 45 degrees away from your serving target (fig 8.2R, 8.2L), much as you would if you were throwing a ball at the target. Bend your legs slightly (5-15 degrees at the knees), but no more. You do not want any upward movement when you step and transfer your weight forward.

Start with the foot of your non-serving hand forward. The heel of your front foot should be even with, or just forward of, the toes of your back foot.

FIG 8.2R: _initial posture, right-handers_   _left-handers' initial posture:_ FIG 8.2L

1.   RIGHT-HANDERS (fig 8.2R) - left foot forward.
2.   LEFT-HANDERS (fig 8.2L) - right foot forward.

Some players start with the foot of the non-serving hand back (fig 8.3). They do this to gain additional power when they step to serve. However, this makes the serving action more complex and causes many errors.

non-serving foot back: FIG 8.3

   (a)   (b)   (c)

FIG 8.4: _holding the ball_

Start with the ball at shoulder level, held in your non-serving hand (DO NOT hold the ball with both hands). Let the ball rest in the full length of your fingers when you hold the ball (fig 8.4a). If you hold the ball in your finger tips (fig 8.4b), or if the ball rests in the palm (fig 8.4c), you will have less control when you toss. Your toss will be inconsistent and your serve less accurate.

Think of that point in the air where (AFTER you step) you want to strike the ball (fig 8.5a). Hold the ball directly below that point (fig 8.5b), usually about 6-12 inches forward of your front foot. Holding the ball at this point, your arm should be bent about 15-30 degrees at the elbow.

vertical toss: FIG 8.5

Ideally, you should toss the ball straight up, vertically. If you hold the ball too far forward, you will have to toss it back toward you; hold it too close to your body and you will have to toss it forward.

You will see players who hold the ball with their arm straight, or straighten their arm just before tossing the ball (fig 8.6). Their toss, then, goes up in a circular arc. Depending on when they release the ball, the toss could go forward, or it could drift back behind them.

FIG 8.6: *straight arm toss*

Start with your hand firm and flat, your palm and fingers forming a straight line. Place your hand at the level of the ball. An easy way to do this is to point your fingers at the center of the ball. The forearm of your serving arm should be almost horizontal, with your hand and forearm forming a straight line. Turning your palm slightly outward (thumb down) will help you keep your elbow up and your forearm horizontal.

The Serving Action

Before you start the serving action, you should pull your hitting hand away from the ball, back into position to start the swing. Pull your hitting hand back slowly, keeping the forearm horizontal so that your hitting hand remains forward of the elbow. This will maximize your shoulder rotation (and, thus, your power) during the armswing.

123

FIG 8.7: *pull, then lift and step*

When your hitting hand is about even with your face (fig 8.7):
1) LIFT the ball straight up (slowly), and
2) STEP with your front foot (the foot of your non-hitting hand).
Lift and step at the same time, in one motion. The rhythm for the serving action is PULL . . . then LIFT-and-STEP . . . then SWING. Your toss should be low and precise, the serving action synchronized with the toss.

THE TOSS   The toss is arguably the most important factor in serving technique. When every toss goes to the same place, you can serve with power and control. When your toss is erratic, you lose accuracy and consistency.

The ideal toss should leave the ball sitting in the air, motionless. Serving, then, is like hitting a ball off a batting tee. You would never have to adjust your swing to reach for the ball.

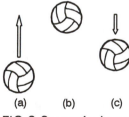

(a)   (b)   (c)

FIG 8.8: *vertical toss*

This happens when your toss is exactly vertical. The ball rises straight up (fig 8.8a). Gravity stops its upward flight, then it descends straight down (fig 8.8c). At the peak of the toss (fig 8.8b), the ball is no longer rising, but not yet falling. It hangs in the air, motionless. Make your toss so that it peaks at exactly the point where you want to strike the ball.

Generally, the ball should only rise about 6-12 inches out of your hand (fig 8.9). A long, slow lift is more accurate than a short, quick motion. Be careful that you do not lower your hand before you toss. Just lift the ball straight up; when your hand stops, the ball will rise out of your hand. DO NOT use any wrist action when you release the ball. You do not want to flip the ball back toward you.

low toss: FIG 8.9

124

When you toss the ball forward or back toward you (or to the right or left), you must adjust your armswing to reach for the ball. Changing your armswing changes the direction of the serve and, usually, puts spin on the ball.

A common error in serving is tossing the ball higher than necessary. A high toss, of course, is usually less accurate. It also disrupts the timing of the serving action. The player tosses, then must wait for the ball to fall before swinging. Often, a high toss is made to accomodate poor serving mechanics.

Some players, for example, toss the ball with both hands (fig 8.10). Tossing with both hands delays the serving action. The toss must be higher, high enough to allow the striking hand to complete the toss, then move back into position and swing. This action is less efficient and creates inconsistency.

FIG 8.10: *tossing with both hands*

A similar situation occurs when a server tosses before pulling the hitting hand back (fig 8.11). The armswing is delayed until the hitting can be pulled back. Because the armswing is delayed, the server must toss the ball higher.

toss ... then pull: FIG 8.11

125

WEIGHT SHIFT   Coordinate the serving action so that you strike the the ball at the peak of the toss, when the ball hangs motioless in the air (fig 8.12). To strike the ball at its peak, step and shift your weight forward as you lift the ball, well before the ball leaves your hand.

FIG 8.12: *weight transfer, during the lift and step*

Take a fairly short step (6-12 inches), directly toward the target of your serve. Just as you would when throwing a ball, shift your weight forward and rotate your hips and shoulders so thay come around to face the target. The more power you need for the serve, the more powerful this step should be.

Some players walk into the serve, taking a step or two before starting the serving action (fig 8.13). Their hips and shoulders start facing the net. Then, during the last step, they must rotate their body back around to the traditional throwing posture. Then, they rotate back to the target as they swing.

FIG 8.13: *walking into the serve*

We DO NOT recommend this method, even though the steps may generate a little more power. The serving action involves far too much hip rotation. Accuracy and consistency are traded for a small increase in power.

126

Many younger players toss the ball by pushing upward (instead of forward) with their legs (fig 8.14). This usually results in an inaccurate toss. Standing straight up during the toss also delays the serving action. Once the toss is completed, the player must regain balance, then step and shift the weight forward. All this must occur before they can swing. The toss, then, must be much higher.

FIG 8.14: *using the legs to toss*

A similar situation occurs when a player waits until the toss is completed before stepping. Perhaps they are waiting to see where the ball goes before stepping (instead of lifting the ball to a precise spot, as recommended). However, stepping after the toss delays delays the armswing, so the player must toss the ball higher to compensate. The end result is a less accurate toss, and a less consistent serve.

ARMSWING   The recommended serving armswing is very similar to the recommended spiking armswing. When you spike, you want to hit the ball topspin; you curve your fingers and snap your wrist. When serving a 'floater', however, you do not want the ball to spin.

Make sure that you DO NOT snap your your wrist or turn your hand when you swing. In addition to putting spin on the ball, turning your wrist will change the direction of the serve. Throughout the serving action, keep your wrist locked and your hitting hand flat.

As you bring your hitting arm away from the ball, the forearm should be almost horizontal, with the hand forward of your elbow. As you step and transfer your weight forward, drive your upper arm and elbow forward; your hitting hand and forearm should rotate to the rear of the elbow. As your upper arm moves forward, your forearm and hitting hand drive up and forward, into contact with the ball (fig 8.15). Your hitting hand should move to the ball in a nearly straight line, not a circular arc.

FIG 8.15: *the recommended armswing*

You should contact the ball directly above, or just in front of, your hitting shoulder. Contact the ball high above your shoulder, though not as high as you can reach. A high contact point allows you to serve with a flatter trajectory; a slightly lower contact gives you a little more power and control.

Some players bring their hitting hand back (instead of the elbow) to start the swing (fig 8.16). Like the similar spiking armswing, the result is a short, compact swing. As with the spike, this swing generates far less power. Some servers have enough power so that this is not a problem. For others, it can be detrimental. The recommended armswing will provide more power and, often, more control.

FIG 8.16: *short, compact armswing*

FIG 8.17: *long, looping armswing*

You will find players who bring their hitting hand well below the shoulder, (fig 8.17). This results in a long, circular armswing, similar to the looping armswing used by some spikers. The circular armswing is longer and less consistent than a straight line swing. The erratic serving action makes the serve difficult to control. In addition, it often puts spin on the ball.

Contact Surface

The portion of the hand that strikes the ball should form a hard, flat contact surface (fig 8.18). Lock your wrist so that your fingers, palm, and forearm form a straight line. Spread the fingers slightly, about one half inch or less.

Strike the ball with the lower third of the palm area. Keep your lower palm flat and firm. DO NOT curve you fingers. Curving your fingers will give you a rounded contact surface, which could put spin on the ball. If your fingers are curved, they are more likely to contact the ball, and put spin on the serve.

Tense your hand and fingers as you form the striking surface. The firmer you make your hand, of course, the more power you deliver to the ball. Some

contact area: FIG 8.18

players keep their hand relaxed, then form the contact surface just before contact. You will find it much easier to form the striking hand early, as you take your initial posture. Then, just maintain it throughout the serving action.

Contact the ball at the center of the ball's surface. Striking the ball above (or below) its center causes the serve to go downward (or up). Hitting the left (or right) side of the ball sends the serve to the right (or left), instead of to the target.

Follow-through

Follow-through in the serving action is undesirable. It contributes no power, and usually causes the ball to spin. Stop your hand immediately when you contact the ball (fig 8.19). Make sure, however, that you DO NOT slow your hand before striking the ball. Just do not continue forward after you make contact.

FIG 8.19: *NO follow-through*

THE UNDERHAND SERVE

You'll spend most of your volleyball life using an overhand serve. Why, then, should you learn an underhand serve? There are several reasons we use underhand serves in learning situations, not the least of which is that it is an easier serve to pass. In instructional settings, underhand serves provide more opportunities to pass, set, and spike, and to block and dig. The underhand serve can also be a valuable lead-up to learning the mechanics of the overhand serve.

Some players, until they master an efficient technique, lack the strength to serve overhand with power and accuracy. Younger players, especially, may not have developed the muscular strength needed to serve overhand effectively. The mechanics of the underhand technique presented here (fig 8.20, next page) are very similar to those of the overhand serve. You can learn and practice many important aspects of the overhand technique while serving underhand.

FIG 8.20: *the underhand serve*

Initial Posture

Take a stance similar to that described for the overhand serve. Turn farther away from the serving target, more toward the sideline. Place your feet about shoulder width apart:
1)   RIGHT-HANDERS (fig 8.21R) - left foot forward
2)   LEFT-HANDERS (fig 8.21L) - right foot forward

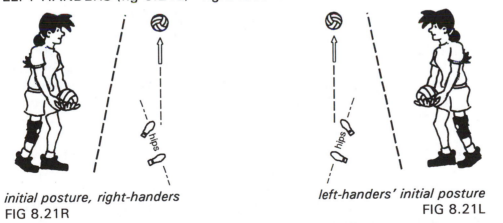

initial posture, right-handers
FIG 8.21R

left-handers' initial posture
FIG 8.21L

Hold the ball just below waist level, about 6-12 inches forward of the front hip. Place your hitting hand near the ball, bending your arm slightly (15-30 degrees at the elbow). Your hitting hand should be flat and firm.

131

The Serving Action

Pull your hitting arm back BEFORE you lift the ball. Keep the hitting arm bent slightly as you bring the hand away from the ball (fig 8.22). The bent arm gives you a shorter, more accurate striking lever, similar to using a shorter bat in softball. DO NOT straighten the arm as you bring your hand back to serve.

pulling the hand: FIG 8.22

FIG 8.23: *lift and step*

THE TOSS   The rhythm for the lift, step, and swing is very similar to that described for the overhand serve. As your hitting arm moves back 12-18 inches (about even with your hip), lift the ball and step forward (fig 8.23). Lift the ball straight up; DO NOT toss the ball forward, out in front of you.

Lift the ball slowly, NOT quickly. The ball should rise only 2-4 inches out of your hand when you stop the lifting action. As with the overhand serve, tossing the ball too high is a very common error. The toss should peak at the exact point where you want to strike the ball, usually just above waist level.

Your serve trajectory will reflect any inaccuracies in your toss. If your toss is too high, your serve is likely to go up toward the ceiling. A toss that is too far forward usually results in a low trajectory serve, one that often winds up in the net. Of course, when the ball only goes 2-4 inches out of your hand, you should have an accurate toss.

WEIGHT TRANSFER   As with the overhand serve, step and shift your weight forward as you begin to lift the ball (fig 8.24, below). This step should be short (6-12 inches) and controlled. The weight transfer should move your body forward, directly toward the target, NOT upward.

FIG 8.24: *the serving action (underhand)*

THE SWING   As you step, swing your hitting hand into contact with the ball (fig 8.24, above). As with the overhand serve, swing your hand in a nearly straight line, not a circular loop. A looping swing sends the ball upward.

Lock your wrist; keep your hand and forearm in a straight line throughout the swing. Keep your elbow slightly bent, and locked as well. If you bend your elbow further (during the swing), the serve is likely to go straight up, toward the ceiling.

Contact Surface

Shape your hand exactly as you would for the overhand serve. Not only will you have a flat contact surface, but you will also be reinforcing the learning of the overhand serve. Contact the ball with the lower third of the heel area. Make sure that the fingers do not contact the ball.

You'll see many different hand shapes used by underhand servers: cupped hand, curved hand, fist and half-fist. Though these may work for some servers, they do not always form a flat contact surface. And, they may not work so well when the player begins serving overhand.

Key Points - Overhand serve

INITIAL POSTURE
1. Start with the foot of your NON-serving hand forward:
2. Hold the ball
    a. at about the level of your shoulders,
    b. slightly forward of your front foot (6-12 inches),
3. Your serving arm
    a. should be at the height of the held ball,
    b. with your forearm almost horizontal;
4. COMMON ERRORS
    a. holding the ball too low, or with the arm straight.

THE SERVING ACTION
The serving sequence is: (1) pull, (2) lift and step, (3) swing.
1. PULL your serving arm straight back, slowly; keep your forearm horizontal.
2. LIFT, when your hitting hand is 12-18 inches back, away from the ball:
    a. slowly lift the ball straight up (vertically) using no wrist action;
    b. the ball should peak only 6-12 inches above head level;
    STEP at the same time your hand is lifting the ball,
    a. the step should be a short step (6 to 12 inches);
    b. shift your weight forward, onto your front foot;
3. SWING as your weight shifts forward.
    a. The swing is similar to the spiking armswing, but with no wrist snap:
    b. your hitting hand moves in a nearly straight line, not in an arc;
4. COMMONS ERRORS
    a. tossing the ball too high,
    b. mistiming the toss-and-step sequence,
    c. pushing upward with the legs during the toss.

CONTACT SURFACE
1. Keep your striking hand firm and flat;
    a. your fingers should be straight, NOT cupped or curved;
    b. your forearm, palm, and fingers should form a straight line;
2. Strike the ball with the lower third of the palm area.
3. Keep your wrist locked before, during, or after contact.
4. COMMON ERRORS
    a. snapping the wrist.

FOLLOW-THROUGH
1. Stop your hand as soon as it contacts the ball.
2. Be careful that your hand does not slow down before contact.

Key Points - Underhand serve

The underhand technique recommended here is very similar to the overhand technique described previously. Modify the overhand technique as follows:

INITIAL POSTURE:
1. The line between the shoulders should be pointed toward the target area.
2. Place the ball
    a. just below waist level,
    b. just forward of your front hip (6-12 inches).
3. Your serving arm
    a. the serving arm should be bent slightly;
    b. your hand and forearm should be in a straight line,
4. COMMON ERRORS
    a. facing the target,
    b. holding the ball too close to the body, or too far forward.

THE SERVING ACTION
1. PULL
    a. Slowly pull your serving hand back, away from the ball;
    b. keep your elbow bent 15-30 degrees.
2. LIFT the ball, slowly
    a. the ball should rise only a few inches out of your hand, peaking about waist level.
    STEP (a short step)
    a. at the same time your hand is lifting the ball,
    b. directly at the target of your serve.
3. SWING as your weight shifts forward, near the end of your step:
    a. keep your elbow slightly bent and locked during the swing;
    b. move your hand forward in a straight line, not in a circular loop.
4. COMMON ERRORS
    a. pushing upward with the legs during the toss,
    b. tossing the ball too high,
    c. bending the elbow during the swing.

BLOCKING

A team moves to their defensive mode when they send the ball to the other team, whether by serving, spiking, or just volleying the ball across the net. When a team shifts to defense, the front row players become blockers and move to the net. Generally, they should be in position before the opposing team passes the ball.

In the act of blocking, the blockers try to prevent an opponent's attack from crossing the net (fig 9.1). Blocking is the first line of a team's defense. It is also the cornerstone of a team's backcourt defense.

FIG 9.1: *blocking*

The technique information that follows in this chapter applies to blockers in general. Often, middle blockers must modify this technique to meet the demands of defending quick attacks and ranging far to oppose the outside attack. Where the techniques for middle and outside blockers differ, those differences will be noted.

Starting Position

Each front row player is assigned an are where they block. The most common alignment places the setters or 'opposite' players on the right side. The taller blockers are positioned in the middle area, leaving the other hitters to block on the left side. There are, of course, many variations, but this is the most common alignment.

Most blockers start near the net, within 1-2 feet (fig 9.2). One of the key factors in blocking success is reaching across the net, penetrating into the opponent's court space to intercept the spike before it crosses the net. Starting close to the net allows the blockers to reach across into the opponent's court as soon as their hands rise above the net.

starting close
FIG 9.2

In recreational play, unskilled players sometimes start away from the net, then run forward to block. Usually, they do this to gain momentum for the jump, similar to a spike approach. However, the blocker who runs forward is usually not very effective, even though they might jump an inch or two higher:

1) their arms are too far from the net; the ball is usually blocked down onto the blocker's side of the net.

2) timing the block is much more difficult;

3) low sets are often hit before the blocker can move forward and jump.

You will be a much more effective blocker if you start near the net, even if you do not jump quite as high.

MIDDLE BLOCKERS   From their starting positions, blockers sometimes move to another area to block. If a hitter moves to another area, for example, the blocker may be required to move along with the hitter (this may or may not be the case, depending on the defensive system being used).

Middle blockers are often required to adjust their initial position. The opponent's quick attack may not occur exactly in the center area. The middle blocker must move (BEFORE the setter receives the pass) into position to oppose the quick attack. From this position, they must still be able to move and defend against other attacks.

Initial Posture

In their initial posture, blockers should be balanced and stable, ready to move quickly to the right or the left (fig 9.3). As a blocker, start with your hips and shoulders parallel to the net. Place your feet about shoulder width apart, or slightly more. Turn your feet slightly inward and shift your weight forward to the balls of your feet. Bend your knees about 30-45 degrees.

Start with your hands to the side and slightly forward of your shoulders, within 8-12 inches of the net. From this position, you can drive your hands up and across the net very quickly. Remember, however, that your hands are starting farther apart than the width of the ball. You must bring your hands closer together (to about 8 inches apart) before they rise above the net.

initial blocking posture: FIG 9.3

FIG 9.4: *hands too low*

Inexperienced players often start with their hands at waist level, or even lower. They jump and swing their arms up in circular motion, bringing their hands into blocking position at the end of the arc (fig 9.4). Their hands remain well apart until the last moment. Naturally, many spikes go between their arms, spikes that would otherwise be blocked.

To prevent the ball from going between the hands or arms, some players start with their hands about 6 inches apart, directly in front of their chest (fig 9.5). This allows their hands to remain close together as they drive them up to block. However, the arms are cramped in this initial position, slowing the upward movement of the hands and arms. For that reason, we do not recommend this position.

hands close together
FIG 9.5

139

MIDDLE BLOCKERS   When you defend quick attacks, as middle blockers often do, you need to elevate and place your hands above the net quickly. This is often more important than how high you jump. Start with your hands up around head level (fig 9.6), or higher. From this posture, as soon as you leave the ground, your hands will be in blocking position. Keep in mind, however, that you cannot jump as high, or move as quickly, from this posture. When there is no quick attack, start with your hands about shoulder level.

middle blocker
FIG 9.6

FOCUS OF ATTENTION   The following is a typical attention sequence used by both middle and outside blockers:

1) BEFORE THE PASS is made:
    a)   identify all of your opponent's available hitters;
    b)   quickly identify the location of the pass.
2) While the PASS IS IN THE AIR (well before the setter receives the ball):
    a)   track the movement of the spikers, especially those approaching near your area of coverage;
    b)   move into position opposite the quick attack, if that is your responsibility; then,
    c)   focus on the setter and determine the location of the set.

Effective blockers identify where the set is going very quickly. They do this by focusing their attention on the setter; they DO NOT watch the ball. Setters often show their set selection. Some setters, for example, contact the ball higher when setting quick sets; some arch their back early when making a backset. Watch the setter and you can get an early indication of the set.

When you know the direction of the set, move toward the attack. As you move (during the first 3-5 feet of the ball's flight), determine the speed of the set, and the location of the attack. There is nothing more you can gain from watching the ball; turn your attention to the spiker. Hitters often show their spike direction, in the same way that setters 'telegraph' their set selection.

Study the hitter's approach and jump while you move into blocking position, and block accordingly. For example, a hitter moving radically in from the sideline is likely to hit a cross-court spike; block their angle. Many hitters turn to face the direction they intend to hit; block that direction. You will not notice any of this, of course, if you are looking at the ball.

DO NOT watch the ball. This is a very difficult thing for blockers to learn, but it is among the most important. Once you know where the set is going, focus on the spiker; DO NOT look back to the ball.

140

Movement to Alignment (Outside Blockers)

Outside blockers are generally responsible for 'setting the block'; they establish the location of the block. The middle blocker moves to a position alongside the outside blocker so that they jump and block together.

As an outside blocker, you should identify the set and move into blocking position very quickly, not at the last minute. If you move too late, or too slow, you may interfere with the middle blocker's movement to the outside. Even though you might arrive in time to block, you could cause your middle blocker to be late, or out of position.

Outside blockers seldom have to cover more than 4-6 feet to be in position to block. It is much too complex and time consuming to turn and run such a short distance, then turn back and prepare to jump. Instead of turning and running, use one or two slide steps (fig 9.7L, 9.7R). You can cover the distance quickly, while keeping your body aligned and postured for the blocking action.

NET ———————————————— 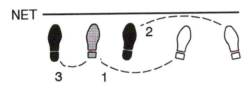 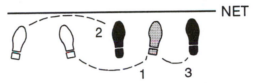 ———————————————— NET

FIG 9.7L: *slide steps, moving left*   *slide steps, moving right:* FIG 9.7R

Take your 1st step (lead foot) with the foot closest to the attack. This step can be a long step, or a short step, depending on the distance you need to cover. Take your 2nd step by moving your trail foot alongside the lead foot. Immediately, almost before your trail foot settles to the floor, move your lead foot again (3rd step). Place your lead foot so that your feet are positioned to jump (fig 9.7). Usually, this is about shoulder width apart.

FIG 9.7: *slide steps*

141

DO NOT wait until you are in blocking position before preparing for the blocking action. Prepare to jump and block as you move to the attack:
1)   Keep your hips and shoulders parallel to the net;
2)   keep your hands at about shoulder level,
3)   held fairly close to the net (8-12 inches).
4)   During your last two steps, bend your legs to about 90-110 degrees.
Again, as you move into blocking position, study the hitter's approach, jump, and armswing. DO NOT watch the ball.

Alignment (Outside Blockers)

Outside spikers generally start their approach as the ball is set. As an outside blocker, you should identify the set quickly, then focus on the hitter. Move quickly and position the block in front of the hitter's hitting shoulder.

Reach the point of attack BEFORE the hitter. Think of a basketball game where a player dribbles to the baseline. The defender tries to cut off the player's lane to the basket. The defender does not move alongside the offensive player; the defender moves into the path of the dribbler, getting there before the dribbler does. In the same way, you as a blocker should move in front of the hitter, blocking the path of the attack.

A team's defensive strategy determines the exact placement of the block. Blocking the center court area is a common strategy against typical sets, those where the ball is 2-4 feet from the net. The block allows a narrow lane for both the down-the-line and cross-court spikes (fig 6.8a). The theory, of course, is that it is easier to defend (and harder to hit) two small lanes than one larger area. As an outside blocker, set the block by positioning your outside arm just inside the hitting shoulder of the spiker (fig 9.8b).

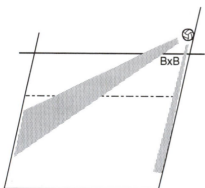

FIG 9.8a: *typical set (2-4 feet)*

FIG 9.8b: *blocking the center court area*

142

Another scheme is to block one path, usually the hitter's best shot, leaving a wider area unblocked. This can be your primary strategy, but it is usually most effective when the set favors a specific attack or, conversely, the set limits the hitter's options.

When the ball is set close to the net (within 0-2 feet), for example, a hitter can easily hit the ball at a sharp downward angle, too sharp for the backcourt defender to handle. In such a case, the blockers should block the down-the-line area (fig 9.9a). As an outside blocker, place your chest directly across from the hitting shoulder of the spiker (fig 9.9b).

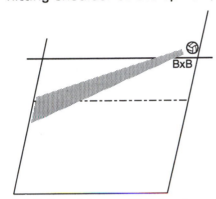

FIG 9.9a: *tight set (0-2 feet)*

FIG 9.9b: *blocking the line area*

When the ball is set far away from the net (5 feet or more), however, the down-the-line spike is a more difficult shot. The hitter is more likely to hit the ball deep into the cross-court area. As an outside blocker, then, move the block more inside (fig 9.10a). Do this by placing your outside arm well inside of the spiker's hitting shoulder: the deeper the set, the more inside you should move the block (fig 9.10b).

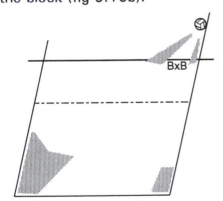

FIG 9.10a: *deep sets (5 feet or more)*

FIG 9.10b: *blocking more of the angle*

143

Before the play, note whether the opposing hitter is right-handed or left-handed. Set the block by placing your outside blocking arm in relation to the spiker's hitting arm, NOT his or her body.

Let's say that you are blocking on your team's right side. To block the down-the-line spike, line up your outside blocking arm directly across from the spiker's hitting shoulder. Notice how your blocking position in relation to their body is different for a left-handed spiker than it is for a right-handed hitter.

1) RIGHT-HANDED HITTER (9.11a): slightly inside from the hitter's body;
2) LEFT-HANDED HITTER (9.11b): slightly outside from the hitter's body.

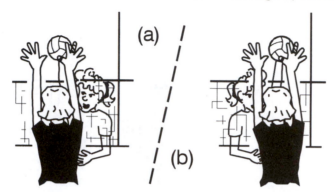

FIG 9.11: *blocking the down-the-line spike*

To block the cross-court, line up your outside blocking arm just inside from their hitting shoulder. Again, your blocking position relative to the hitter's body will be different for left-handers than it is for right-handers.

1) RIGHT-HANDED HITTER (9.12c): completely inside from the hitter's body;
2) LEFT-HANDED HITTER (9.12d): almost directly across from the hitter.

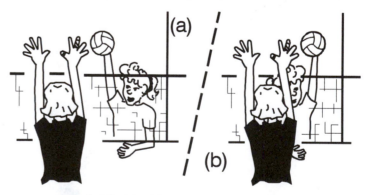

FIG 9.12: *blocking the cross-court spike*

The same would be true if you were blocking on your team's left side, or even in the middle. Always set the block relative to the spiker's hitting shoulder.

144

Outside blockers sometimes wind up blocking alone. This can occur when the middle blocker overly commits to the quick attack, or when an opponent uses a very fast set to the outside. When blocking alone, position your block so that you take away the opposite corner (fig 9.13). Your backcourt defense, then, can place two players on each side of the block.

If the set is close to the net (within 1-2 feet), as it often is, block more of the down-the-line area. On a tight set, the closeness of the set will usually restrict all but the sharpest of cross-court spikes.

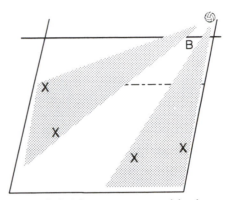

FIG 9.13: *one-person block*

Movement to Alignment (Middle Blockers)

Middle blockers generally oppose every attack, blocking all along the net. Before the setter receives the pass, the middle blocker should move to the area of the opponent's middle attacks (Note: this is NOT always the exact middle). From this position, the middle blocker may have to move 10-12 feet, or farther, to reach the outside attack. Of course, the attack could be much closer.

Middle blockers can cover short distances using the same slide-step pattern used by outside blockers (fig 9.7, page ???). Covering longer distances, however, slide steps may be too slow. When moving to the outside, middle blockers more often use the 3-step crossover pattern (fig 6.14R, 9.14L). Crossover steps allow the middle blocker to turn and run to the outside, while keeping the upper body postured to start the blocking action.

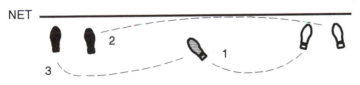

FIG 9.14L: *crossover steps, moving left*

crossover steps, moving right: FIG 9.14R:

145

Using the crossover pattern (fig 9.14, below), the 1st step is always taken with the foot nearest the attack location (the lead foot). Your 1st step should be a LONG step. A short step may feel more natural; it may even seem quicker. However, it will be difficult reaching the outside attack in three steps if you take a short first step.

Turn your hips in the direction of the run as you take your 1st step. Your shoulders should remain nearly parallel (within 15-30 degrees) to the net, with your outside hand fairly close to the net (within 8-12 inches). This will ensure that your arms are close to the net when you reach the attack. Make sure that you DO NOT drift away from the net as you move to the outside.

FIG 9.14: *3-step crossover*

Your 2nd step should be long enough to take you to the attack. Plant this foot (your trail foot) with a heel-to-toe action similar to a that of a spiker. As your trail foot touches down, your toe should be pointing back toward the net. This allows your hips to rotate back around and face the net during your last step. Pointing your foot toward the sideline will prevent your hips from rotating back around to face the net, causing you to face the out-of-bounds area as you jump.

As your 2nd step lands, you should start bending your legs for the jumping action, just as you do at the end of your spike approach. By the time your 3rd step lands, your knees should be bent about 75-90 degrees and you should be ready to jump and block (fig 9.14a). This, of course, is much faster than running to the outside position . . . then getting ready to jump. In addition to being faster, you can gain valuable inches by making your movement and blocking jump one continuous action, just as the energy of the spike approach helps you jump higher.

FIG 9.14a

146

As you are taking your 2nd step (trail foot), usually before this foot returns to the floor, start your 3rd step (the lead foot). The last two steps (2nd and 3rd) resembles the step-plant of a hitter's approach: there is a distinct one ... two sequence to the landing. The sequence should be very fluid: 1st step, 2nd and 3rd steps. It should NOT be 1st step . . . then 2nd step . . . then 3rd step.

You should be ready to jump as your 3rd step (lead foot) touches down. Plant this foot so that your feet are about shoulder width apart, with the outside foot a little closer (1-3 inches) closer to the net. Do not use the heel-to-toe plant for this step. Instead, plant on the balls of your foot. This helps you control your momentum, and increases your stability.

Many blockers lose valuable time because of their footwork. In trying to move quickly, they take short steps. Then, they cannot reach the outside attack in three steps. Often, these blockers cover the remaining distance by adding a hop onto the end of their movement (fig 9.15L, 9.15R). This pattern (NOT recommended here) is 1st step, 2nd step, hop onto both feet (fig 9.15).

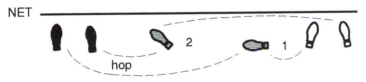

FIG 9.15L: *moving left with a hop*

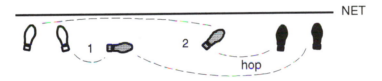

FIG 9.15R: *moving right, with a hop*

FIG 9.15: *3-step with a hop*

147

The hop takes additional time, but this is not the only disadvantage. Players who hop at the end of their movement are less balanced and have less stability when they jump. This not only costs them jumping power, it causes them to 'float' as they block. Often, they float past the attack, crashing into the outside blocker (fig 9.16). Sometimes they even float forward into the net.

FIG 9.16: *'crashing'*

The 3-step pattern previously described is much preferred. As a middle blocker, learn to use long enough strides to reach the outside attack areas in the three steps. Practice your footwork so that you can build speed and jumping power using this simple and effective pattern.

As you move into blocking position, DO NOT watch the ball. Focus your attention on the following:
1) the initial flight of the set (3-5 feet),
2) the position of the outside blocker,
3) the approach and body language of the hitter;

Alignment (Middle Blockers)

The middle blocker is a team's primary defense against quick-tempo attacks. A quick attack gives a blocker only enough time to jump and penetrate; you will not usually have time to adjust your position once the ball is set.
1) BEFORE the set (while the pass is the air),
   a) read the approach path of the middle hitter;
   b) position yourself in front of the hitter's path;
   c) then, look back to the setter and read the set.
2) DURING the set, locate the attack (the set location):
   a) jump and block if they set the quick attack;
   b) move to the attack and block if they set the ball to another hitter.

When blocking middle attacks, you will usually align your chest directly across from the spiker's hitting shoulder (fig 9.17, next page). This takes away the center of the court and forces the hitter to turn their spike. Of course, this is only a general alignment.

148

Your exact alignment could vary depending on:
1) the hitter's tendencies (i.e., their favorite shot),
2) the angle of the approach,
3) the turn of the body,
4) the position of the ball relative to the hitting shoulder.

If the set goes to the outside area, instead of the middle, react quickly and move to join the outside blocker. Time your movement so that you and your blocking partner jump together. Both blockers should have their hands in blocking position when the spiked ball nears the net.

FIG 9.17: *blocking the quick attack*

A situation that often occurs in recreational play (and, surprisingly, even in competition) is that the ball is set too far inside (fig 9.18a). The attack is designed for the outside attack area, but the set does not have enough power to reach the sideline. The ball winds up falling 6-8 feet inside from the sideline.

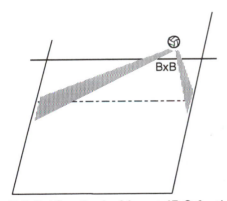

FIG 9.18a: *far inside set (5-8 feet)*

FIG 9.18b: *middle blocker sets the block*

When this occurs, you (as a middle blocker) may be closer to the attack than the outside blocker. If you were to move completely to the outside blocker, you would probably overrun the attack, leaving the hitter's best shot (the cross-court angle) uncovered. Instead of closing to the outside blocker, move into position to block the cross-court spike (fig 9.18b). This leaves the outside blocker enough room to move alongside your block.

The Blocking Action

As you reach the attack, your posture should be as follows (fig 9.19):

1) your hips and shoulders should be parallel to the net;
2) your feet should be shoulder width apart, your knees bent 75-90 degrees;
3) your back should be straight, and leaning only slightly forward;
4) your hands at shoulder level, within 8-12 inches of the net;

ready to jump and block: FIG 9.19

Make sure that your hips and shoulders are parallel to the net before you jump. You should be watching the hitter; but, DO NOT turn your shoulders to face that direction. Many inexperienced blockers make the mistake of facing the hitter when they jump to block. Then, when they block the ball, it flies out of bounds (fig 6.20).

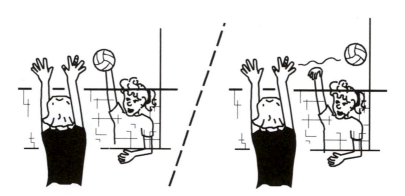

FIG 9.20: *blocker facing the hitter*

The blocking action for both outside and middle blockers is similar (fig 9.21, below). The first phase of the blocking action is the jump. Time your jump so that your hands are at their greatest height and penetration as the spiked ball reaches the net area. Jump according to the jump of the hitter:

1) TIGHT SETS (1-2 feet), jump as the spiker jumps.
2) TYPICAL SETS (2-5 feet), jump just after the spiker jumps.
3) DEEP SETS (5 feet or more), jump later than the spiker (the deeper the set, the later you jump).

FIG 9.21: *the blocking action*

Usually, you will arrive in position to block with your legs bent 45-90 degrees. Start your jump by dipping a little lower, to a knee angle of about 90-110 degrees. This 'loads' your muscles; it stretches them and intensifies your explosive power. As you jump, keep your back straight and your torso only slightly forward (0 to 15 degrees). DO NOT arch your back when you jump. If you arch your back, you will pull your torso and your arms away from the net.

As you jump, and throughout the blocking action, keep your hands and arms fairly close to the net (within 8 inches). The ball, then, cannot fit between your arms and the net. When your arms are farther away from the net, the spiker can drive the ball between your arms and the net. The ball falls to your side of the court, costing your team the point or side-out opportunity.

As you jump, drive your arms directly up to the top of the net. As you continue rising, extend your hands above and across the net. Penetrate across the net as far as you can reach without touching the net. Make sure that your hands are turned in, facing the center of your opponent's court. Any movement of your hands and arms during the blocking action should be towards the center of your opponent's court.

A common error among many blockers (especially outside blockers) is to reach to the outside (toward the sideline) when they see the spiker hitting the ball down-the-line. As an outside blocker, you should almost never reach outside your body to 'chase' the hitter. This seldom results in a good block. Most often, you block the ball out of bounds. If the hitter turns the spike outside your block, you should just rely on your down-the-line digger to keep the ball in play.

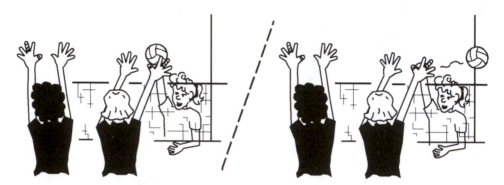

FIG 9.22: *'chasing' the hitter*

The movement of your hands above and across the net should be one smooth, fluid motion. Inexperienced blockers often make this two separate movements, up . . . then forward (fig 6.23). If you do this, your hands remain too far from the net until the arms move forward and close the gap. Often, the balls you block will fall down your side of the net. In addition, aggressively pressing the arms forward could cause you to contact the net.

FIG 9.23: *two separate motions, up ... then across*

Contact with the Ball

You will block most balls with your hands, though some may be blocked by your arms. Before you rise above the net, turn your hands (especially your outside hand) in toward your opponent's court. Reach a little further across the net with your outside hand. This will turn your hands, and your arms as well, in toward the court. Do these two things and most of your blocks will go back at your opponents, rather than out of bounds.

You want your hands to cover a large area, but you want them to be strong enough to deflect the hardest of spikes. Generally, spread your fingers about one-half to one inch; spread your thumbs about an inch or two from your fingers (fig 9.24a). If you keep your fingers closer together, you'll have strength, but not much coverage (fig 9.24b). If you spread your fingers too much, you'll have more coverage, but little strength . . . you will also have banged up fingers (fig 9.24c). Spread your fingers, but not too much. Keep your hands firm and strong.

(a): *recommended*   (b): *fingers too close*   (c): *fingers too spread*
FIG 9.24

From the time you rise above and penetrate the net, have your hands fairly close together. Having them close together will prevent the ball to from going between your hands. Many players block with their hands too far apart. A spiker can drive the ball between the hands any time they are further apart than the width of the ball (about 8 inches).

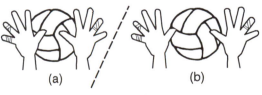

(a)   (b)

FIG 9.25

Follow-Through

Once your blocking action ends, make sure your follow-through does not bring your arms or hands into the net. Hang in the air and maintain your block until your body starts to fall. When your body begins to descend, move your arms back to your side of the net. Many blockers contact the net because they bring their hands immediately down to their sides. You can avoid this by first bringing your arms back to vertical, then down to your sides.

FIG 9.26: *follow-through and landing*

You're blocking action seldom ends the play. Once your block ends, you must prepare for your next play:
1)   Bend your knees and use your leg muscles to control your landing.
2)   Pivot in the direction of the spike and find the ball.
3)   Once you know where the ball is, move and prepare for your next play.
4)   Your team's transition strategy, of course, defines your next play.

Key Points

INITIAL POSITION
1.   Move to your blocking position before your opponent passes the ball:
2.   Start close to the net (within 1-2 feet).
3.   COMMON ERRORS
     a.   starting too far away from the net.

INITIAL POSTURE
1.   Start with your hips and shoulders parallel to the net.
2.   Hold your hands:
     a.   at about shoulder height (head height or above for middle blockers),
     b.   slightly outside and in front of your shoulders,
     c.   fairly close to the net (within 8-12 inches).
3.   COMMON ERRORS
     a.   holding the hands too low.

MOVEMENT TO ALIGNMENT (outside blockers)
1.   Use slide-steps to move to the area of the attack.
     a.   keep your hips and shoulders parallel to the net;
     b.   keep your hands at shoulder height and fairly close to the net;
     c.   prepare for the blocking action as you move into position.
2.   Focus your attention on the following:
     a.   the initial flight of the set (3-5 feet), then
     b.   the approach and body language of the hitter,
     c.   DO NOT watch the ball.
3.   COMMON ERRORS
     a.   turning to fact the hitter as you move.
     b.   watching the ball.

ALIGNMENT (outside blockers)
1.   TYPICAL SETS (2-4 feet from the net) - place your outside blocking shoulder just inside the hitting shoulder of the spiker.
2.   TIGHT SETS (less than 2 feet from the net) - place your chest directly across from the hitting shoulder of the spiker.
3.   DEEP SETS (5 feet from the net or more) - place your block more inside the spiker (the deeper the set, the more inside your block).
4.   INSIDE SETS (5-8 feet in from the sideline) - move inside, and position yourself next to your middle blocker.

MOVEMENT TO ALIGNMENT (middle blockers)
1. Use slide-steps when the attack is nearby (within 6-8 feet).
2. When the set goes to the outside, use the 3-step crossover pattern:
   a. keep your shoulders almost parallel to the net (within 30-45 degrees);
   b. keep your outside hand fairly close to the net (within 8-12 inches).
3. Prepare your body to jump during your 2nd and 3rd steps.
   a. bend your legs to jump (about 90-110 degrees at the knee);
   b. bring your hips and shoulders back to parallel with the net;
4. COMMON ERRORS
   a. turning to face the sideline as you move outside;
   b. drifting away from the net a you move outside.

ALIGNMENT (middle blockers)
1. During the pass, align across from the first spiker approaching the middle.
2. Then, before the pass arrives, focus your attention on the setter.
3. As the setter delivers the ball, move in the direction of the set.
   a. MIDDLE ATTACKS - jump, you should already be in position.
   b. OUTSIDE ATTACKS - move alongside the outside blocker.
   c. INSIDE SETS - move into the path of the cross-court spike.

THE BLOCKING ACTION (all blockers)
1. Thrust your hands above and across the net in one fluid motion.
   a. reach as far across the net as your height and jumping ability allow;
   b. turn your hands in toward the center of your opponent's court.
2. Time your jump relative to the jump of the opposing spiker:
   a. TIGHT SETS (1-2 feet) - jump as the hitter jumps.
   b. TYPICAL SETS (2-5 feet) - jump just after the hitter jumps.
   c. DEEP SETS - jump later (the deeper the set, the later you jump).
3. COMMON ERRORS
   a. blocking in two seperate actions: up . . . then across;
   b. reaching outside the body, towards the sideline.

CONTACT WITH THE BALL
1. Spread your fingers slightly, but enough to cover a large area.
2. Your hands should be firm, strong enough to deflect the ball.
3. COMMON ERRORS
   a. hands turned toward the sideline area.

FOLLOW-THROUGH
1. When your body begins to fall, bring your arms back away from the net.
2. Land, gain your balance, then turn and prepare for your next play.

DIGGING

Even great blockers cannot be expected to block every attack. Those balls that elude the block are handled by the backcourt players. To be effective, backcourt positioning must be coordinated with the alignment of the blockers.

FIG 10.1: *digging a spike*

Backcourt defenders use a variation of the forearm technique, known as 'digging', to control and pass the opponent's spike. Powerful spikes travel much too fast for you to handle using the traditional passing technique. The rebound alone would send the ball flying far beyond the playing area. The digging technique allows you to absorb the spike's momentum, pass the ball to a teammate, and create a counterattack.

Ready Position

Each player has a specific 'ready defensive position' in the overall defensive design. Just as a team's blockers move to their respective blocking positions, backcourt defenders move to their 'ready defensive position'. Generally, this occurs when the team sends the ball across the net, be that by serve, spike, or volley.

Backcourt diggers have two responsibilities in their ready positions. They must be ready to retrieve any pass that comes directly back across the net. They should also be ready to play any quick attack such as a 1st-tempo spike or a setter tip.

As a backcourt digger, you should be in a medium digging posture as the pass nears the opposing setter (fig 10.2). You will not have time to get ready once the quick attack or tip is made. Be low enough to play balls near the floor, yet high enough to move quickly and cover longer distances. Hold your arms out away from your body, in digging position.

ready position:
FIG 10.2

Digging Position

Once the opposing setter sets the ball, move to your defensive position. Move quickly and be in position by the time the hitter jumps. You will not dig many spikes if you are still moving when the hitter hits the ball. It is better to be slightly out of position than it is to be still moving as the ball is hit. Of course, it is best to be both in position AND in a stable digging posture.

As with your ready position, your team's defensive system will define your digging position relative to each attack. Do not think of your digging position as covering a spot on the floor; think of it as defending a particular attack (covering the tip, for example). The spot on the floor is merely where that attack is likely to go. Generally, backcourt defenders are positioned to dig:
1) spikes directed around the blocked,
2) balls going over the block,
3) tips near the net area.

As you move into digging position, focus your attention on reading the hitter's approach and jump, just as would if you were blocking. Take into consideration the position of the hitter relative to your blockers (the hitter-blocker configuration). Final defensive positioning is generally determined in accordance with the hitter-blocker configuration. DO NOT watch the ball.

FIG 10.3a: *digging cross-court*

FIG 10.3b: *digging down-the-line*

1) DIGGING SPIKES (fig 10.3): be outside the hitter-blocker configuration (directly in line with the hitter; your blockers will be outside that line.

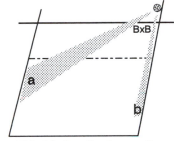

FIG 10.3: *digging spikes*

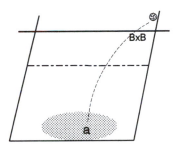

FIG 10.4: *playing deep*

2) BEHIND THE BLOCK (fig 10.4): stay deep in the court, behind the hitter-blocker configuration (the blockers will be between you and the hitter).

FIG 10.4a: *behind the block*

3) COVERING TIPS (fig 10.5): be in the area of the blockers, inside the 3-meter line.

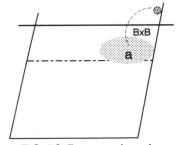

FIG 10.5: *covering tips*

159

Digging Spikes

Whenever you are responsible for digging a direct spike, make sure that there is no one between you and the hitter (see fig 10.3a, 10.3b, previous page). You should have a clear view of the hitter's armswing, and your blockers should be just outside of that view. Since most spikes are directed to the sidelines, you should generally be within a step of the sideline when the spiker hits the ball.

Many diggers read the attack as though there were no blockers present. They move away from the sideline, into the middle court area. Many spikes, then, must be played above the waist, a very difficult ball to handle. It is much more effective to be in a position to dig the ball from below the waist.

DIGGING POSTURE   Spikes can travel at very high speeds, 60-100 miles per hour. Once the ball is hit, you will not have much time to move. You might have time to move a few feet . . . more if the ball is not hit too sharply. Generally, however, you will only have time to step and move your arms in line with the ball once the hitter swings. Backcourt defenders can gain additional time to make the dig by playing the spike later in its flight, when the ball is closer to the floor.

As you prepare to dig a spike, you should be in a fairly low posture, but not too low. Some players get too low when they are in their digging position. Then, they must rise up to meet the ball. Instead of absorbing the energy of the spike, the upward movement adds force to the dig, sending the ball up into the ceiling. In addition, a player that is too low cannot move very fast, or very far.

Try to start at the level of the dig, maybe even a little higher (fig 10.6). By starting higher, you lower your arms when you move to meet the ball. This action absorbs some of the force of the spike. DO NOT, however, use this as an excuse to stand up on defense. You still need to be low enough to extend and play balls near the floor.

Start with your feet a little wider than shoulder width apart; the lower you are, the wider your stance should be. Your weight should be forward, toward the balls of your feet.

digging posture
FIG 10.6

Hold your arms out away from your body as you do when receiving a serve, keeping your upper arms about 30-45 degrees from vertical. Start with your arms bent (30-45 degrees), more than you would if you were receiving a serve. This elbow angle should leave your forearms almost, but not quite, parallel with the floor.

Your hands should be fairly close to gether (6-12 inches apart). If they are too far apart, you might have trouble bringing them together before the spike arrives. However, make sure that you do not join your hands too soon; this would restrict your arms' movement to the ball.

THE DIGGING ACTION   A powerful spike does not give you time to move your body to the ball, then place your arms in position. When digging a powerful spike, move your arms and body simultaneously, at the same time (fig 10.7). Your hands, of course, will move much faster than your whole body. Your arms, then, lead the movement and your body follows. This is exactly the opposite of receiving a serve.

FIG 10.7: *moving to the spike*

Spikes travel at great speed, much faster than serves. If you use the passing technique to dig a spike, the ball will bounce far from your arms . . . MUCH too far. To control the dig, you must absorb the ball's momentum. The digging action recommended here is a modification of the forearm technique designed to handle the spike and control the resulting pass (fig 10.8).

FIG 10.8: *the digging action*

Think of passing a serve. Straightening your arms during the passing action absorbs the ball's momentum; the rebound does not go as far (chapter 3, page 24). When you dig a spike, however, this is exactly what you want to happen.

As you arrive near your digging position, hold your arms away from your body, elbows bent (fig 10.9a). Straighten your arms as you move them to the ball (fig 10.9b). As your arms straighten, the forearms will actually be moving back toward your body. This action is the opposite of moving forward into the ball; it absorbs the energy of the spike, reducing the distance of the rebound.

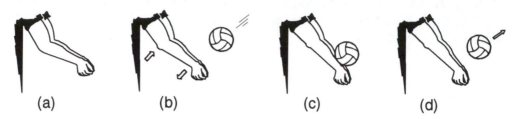

(a)   (b)   (c)   (d)

FIG 10.9: _arm action, absorbing the spike_

Relax your arms. This softens the contact surface, which further decreases the ball's rebound. Be careful, however, that your arms do not recoil back to your body. This would change your arm angle, the likely result being a pass that is too low to handle. At contact, your arms should be about 30-45 degrees from vertical, similar to your passing angle (fig 10.9c).

There are a number of actions that players sometimes use to absorb the spike's force. Some players lean back onto their heels during the digging action (fig 10.10). However, these players generally have a difficult time moving out of this position. Their weight is shifted back, away from the court. They must regain their balance before they can move in another direction. If the ball is hit softly, or deflects off of the block, these players may have difficulty reacting and making a play on the ball.

FIG 10.10: _leaning back during the dig_

Other players thrust their hips forward and arch their back (fig 10.11), using their upper body to absorb the ball. Again, with the weight shifting to the rear, these players have a difficult time reacting to any other play.

FIG 10.11: *arching back during the dig*

Inexperienced players often play defense with their arms close to their body. Then, when they reach for the ball, their arms are moving forward (fig 10.12). The forward motion of the arms adds force to the ball's rebound. The digging action increases the distance of the rebound, sending the ball up into the ceiling or far out of bounds.

FIG 10.12: *arms too close to the body*

Playing Behind the Block

Backcourt defenders playing behind the block are usually shielded (by the blockers) from balls being spiked directly at them. Instead, they cover balls that are arched over the block, or hit deep off of the blocker's hands. Because these balls have less speed than direct spikes, the digger is usually responsible for covering a large area of the court.

INITIAL POSTURE   When playing behind the block, a medium posture will give you excellent mobility and still allow you to play balls near the floor when necessary (fig 10.13). Your posture behind the block should be very similar to your initial posture when receiving a serve.

behind the block
FIG 10.13

Your stance should be fairly wide, with your feet slightly more than shoulder width apart. Generally, your right foot should be forward. Make sure that your hips and shoulders are facing the attack. Your arms should be held so that the passing platform is similar to that used for passing.

In all cases, your attention should be focused on:
1)   the hitter's approach, jump, arm-swing,
2)   the hitter's position relative to your blockers,
3)   NOT the ball.

THE DIGGING ACTION   Generally, spikes going behind the block are deflected up by the blockers. Other balls, such as miss-hit spikes, can also go up and over the block. These will seldom have the same high velocity as typical spikes. Therefore, you will have more time to pursue the ball when you're playing behind the block. Of course, you also have more area to cover.

Balls hit over or deflected up by the block generally have about the same velocity as a serve, sometimes less. Usually, you do not have to be too concerned with absorbing the momentum of the ball. The rebound technique you use to pass a serve is often effective when digging these balls.

Make sure that you first move your body to the shot; then, as you near the ball bring your platform into alignment. DO NOT lead with your arms, letting your body follow.

Sometimes spikers hit the ball over the block at very high speed. This could happen, for example, if you have short blockers. Although you are playing behind the block, you should still use the digging technique previously described to handle these spikes.

Remember, the most effective digs (perhaps the ONLY effective digs) are those that lead to a set and spike of your own. If all you accomplish on defense is to send the ball back over the net, you will not be very successful. Good defense play should result in offensive opportunities.

Key Points

READY POSITION
Generally, move to your 'ready defensive position' when your team sends the ball across the net (by serve, spike, or volley).
1.   As with blocking, be in your 'ready position' before your opponent passes.
2.   Be in a medium posture ready to:
     a.   pass any 1st or 2nd contact being sent across the net, or
     b.   react to and 'dig' a quick attack, or
     c.   move into digging position after the ball is set.
3.   COMMON ERRORS
     a.   standing too upright.

DIGGING POSITION
Your digging position should be coordinated with the alignment of the blockers.
1.   Set your digging position according to the hitter-blocker   configuration:
     DIGGING SPIKES
     a.   do not let the blocker be between you and the hitter;
     BEHIND THE BLOCK
     a.   stay deep, near the end line;
     COVERING TIPS
     a.   move to a position near the blockers and inside the 3-meter line.
2.   Be in position before the hitter jumps.
3.   Watch the hitter, NOT the ball.
4.   COMMON ERRORS
     a.   being too far inside, toward the middle of the court;

INITIAL DIGGING POSTURE
1.   Be in a balanced and stable posture, NOT moving, as the ball is hit.
     DIGGING SPIKES
     a.   be in a low body posture;
     b.   the lower your body, the wider your stance should be.
     PLAYING BEHIND THE BLOCK
     a.   be in a medium body posture,
     b.   spread your feet slightly more than shoulder width apart.
2.   Keep your weight forward, on the balls of your feet.
3.   Hold your arms:
     a.   out in front of your body;
     b.   angle your UPPER arms 30-45 degrees from vertical, similar to passing a serve;

DIGGING SPIKES

a. bend your elbows, 30-45 degrees, so that your FOREARMS are almost horizontal;

BEHIND THE BLOCK

a. bend your elbows, 15-30 degrees, similar to serve reception posture,

4. Focus your attention on:

a. the hitter's approach, jump, arm-swing,

b. the hitter's position relative to the blockers,

c. NOT the ball.

5. COMMON ERRORS

a. still moving when the hitter swings;

b. arms too close to the body.

THE DIGGING ACTION

1. Your initial reaction:

DIGGING SPIKES

a. move your arms and body in line with the flight of the ball;

b. your hands move quicker than your body, so they actually lead the movement and get to the ball first;

c. this is exactly the opposite of passing a serve.

BEHIND THE BLOCK

a. move your body to bring your arms in line with the ball, similar to your passing action.

2. Lower your body by bending at the knees, rather than at the waist.

3. Absorb the force of the spike by straightening your arms as, or just before, you contact the ball.

4. COMMON ERRORS

a. swinging the arms toward the ball;

b. standomg up during the digging action.

DEFENSIVE DESIGN

Team defenses coordinate the efforts of the server, blockers, and diggers to stop, or control, an opponent's attack. The serve attempts to disrupt the opposing offense. The role of the block is to prevent spikes from going into unguarded areas of the team's backcourt. The diggers, then, cover the unblocked areas, receive the spike, and pass the ball so that it can be set. Ultimately, the goal of the defense is to turn an opponent's attack into an attack of their own.

Serving Strategies

Some serving strategies attempt to overpower the receiving team. The server merely goes back and hits their best serve, hoping that the power of the serve is enough to break down the opponent's passing. The jump serve is an example of such a serve.

More commonly, servers attempt to reduce the effectiveness of passers by serving to the team's weak areas. Such strategies include:
1) serving so that a weak passer handles the ball,
2) serving to a weak area in the team's receive formation,
3) or to a location that disrupts their offense plays.

Almost every passing formation includes better passers and weaker passers. The most basic serving strategy is to identify the weakest passers and make them pass the ball; serve directly at them. In addition, the serve can be aimed at a body area where passing is difficult (e.g., serve at their chest).

Every passing formation has strengths and weaknesses. Some formations, for example, are weak in the short middle. Others are weak in the deep middle, or the corners. A serve directed to the vulnerable areas can disrupt a team's passing.

A well placed serve can also disrupt a team's offensive pattern. A short serve (inside the 3-meter line) in the middle may interfere with the team's quick attack, or congest the area. If the quick hitter passes the ball, they will usually be late for the attack. When swing hitters pass from near the net, they may change their spike approach and hit less effectively.

Serving strategy should be a part of the overall defensive design. When the other team passes the ball right to their setter, the blockers and backcourt diggers are at a distinct disadvantage. When the other team passes poorly, however, the defense has a better chance of blocking the attack, or digging the ball and converting it into an offensive play of their own.

Blocking Schemes

Offenses typically have spikers attacking at different tempos and moving to different locations. Blocking schemes are designed to enable blockers to oppose the various options run by an opponent's offense. The goal of the defense is to place two blockers against every attack, leaving no attack unopposed.

MIDDLE BLOCKERS   Middle blockers have two equally important responsibilities. They are often the only blocker opposing attacks (especially quick attacks) in and around the middle area. In addition, they must move and join the outside blocker in opposing attacks from the sideline areas. Essentially, middle blockers are expected to block all along the net, to oppose every attack.

Quick sets do not give a blocker much time. By the time the blocker sees the set . . . then moves to the attacker . . . then jumps to block, it's too late; the hitter will have already hit the ball. The key to blocking quick attacks is to be in position (across from the hitter) BEFORE the ball is set.

Quick hitters generally start their approach when the ball is passed. While the pass is in the air, on its way to the setter, the blocker reads the approach of the quick-hitter, and moves directly across from where he or she will jump (fig 11.1). From this position, the middle blocker should either commit-block or read-block, depending on the team's blocking strategy.

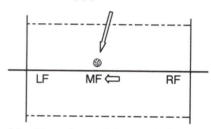

blocking the quick set: FIG 11.1

COMMIT-BLOCKING means that the blocker is committed to stopping the quick attack. As the setter delivers the ball, the blocker jumps along with the hitter. If the set goes to the quick hitter, the blocker is in perfect position for the block. If, however, the set goes to another spiker, the blocker will be in the air with the fake. Usually, there is not have enough time to land . . . then move to the actual attack . . . then jump to block. The outside blockers, then, are left to block alone.

When commit-blocking, the blocker moves to oppose other attacks only when the quick attack is no longer a threat. This could occur early in the play, when the pass is bad, for example. It could also occur late in the play, when the blocker sees the set going to another location.

Commit-blocking is strong against the quick attack, but weak against to outside attacks. It should only be used when an opponent has the ability to score repeatedly with their quick attack.

Many teams are much more effective hitting the slower outside sets than they are hitting the quick attacks. Commit-blocking merely takes away their weakness (the middle), while making their strong suit (the outside attack) even stronger. In most cases, read-blocking is a more effective blocking strategy.

READ-BLOCKING allows the blocker to see the set, and then react in that direction. As before, the blocker moves opposite the attack before the setter receives the pass. From this position, the blocker reacts to the setter and moves in the direction of the set. If the set is to the quick hitter, the blocker jumps (although late, they are already in position). If the set goes to another spiker, the blocker is ready to move and join the outside blocker.

Read-blocking is a strategy that is strong against the outside attack, though less effective against quick-attacks. Many teams use read-blocking as their basic blocking strategy. Then, when an opponent begins having success with the quick attack, they switch to a commit-blocking mode.

OUTSIDE BLOCKERS While middle blockers are expected to block all along the net, outside blockers are more limited in their coverage. Blocking strategies for outside blockers generally fall into one of two areas, zone blocking and man-to-man blocking. A third scheme, stack blocking, is occasionally used in high level competition. It is presented here for information purposes, but it is not recommended for general use.

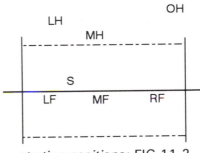

starting positions: FIG 11.2

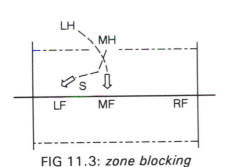

FIG 11.3: *zone blocking*

ZONE BLOCKING schemes (fig 11.3) are the standard strategy for outside blockers. They are the easiest to learn and the simplest to use. Basically, the outside blockers oppose any attacks that occur near to their area. For example, if two hitters were running a crossing play, the outside blocker would block the hitter that crossed into the outside zone. This is similar to using zone coverage football, or playing a zone defense in basketball.

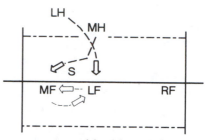

MAN-TO-MAN BLOCKING schemes (fig 11.4) require that outside blockers remain with their hitters, regardless of where those hitters move to attack. In the above example, the blockers would cross along with their respective hitters. This is similar to playing man-to-man defense in basketball, or man pass coverage in football.

man-to-man blocking: FIG 11.4

STACK BLOCKING (fig 11.5) is a complex blocking strategy that is used to block crossing patterns. It allows one blocker to start away from the net, standing behind another blocker (usually the middle blocker). The blocker near the net blocks against quick attack; the 'stack' blocker then moves to block the combination hitter. Because the 'stack' blocker is away from the net, the middle blocker can move anywhere without the middle blocker being in the way.

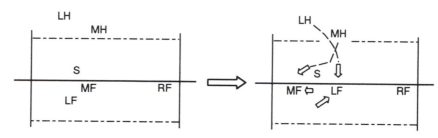

FIG 11.5: *stack blocking*

Basic Defensive Systems

Every defensive scheme must account for the shots spikers hit into the court areas left unguarded by the block. It falls upon the backcourt players to cover these areas, to cover these shots:
1) the down-the-line spike,
2) the cross-court (power angle) spike,
3) balls tipped over the block, and
4) balls driven over the block, or off the blockers' hands, deep into the court.

There are a number of defensive systems used in volleyball play. Teams may use one basic defensive scheme, or combine a number of systems. Most teams make modifications on the systems to fit their philosophy and personnel. What follows are general descriptions of the more common defensive systems.

170

CENTER-UP DEFENSE (fig 11.6)   The center-up defense is frequently found at the lower levels of play. However, it is rarely used in competition, even at moderate levels; at the higher levels, it is virtually nonexistent.

The center-up defense positions the center backrow defender (CB) up near the 3-meter line. From there, they move in the direction of the set and cover tips going over the block. Teams commonly switch the setter to this position so they are in a position to set in transition.

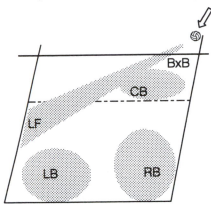

center-up defense: FIG 11.6

The left (LB) and right (RB) backrow players are near the deep corners. They are able to cover a large portion of the court, but only when the ball is not hit too sharply.

The off-blocker (LF) is responsible for digging the cross-court spike. To be in digging position, however, they must move 13-18 feet away from the net.

Generally, the center-up defense is most effective against teams that do not spike with much power, or hit sharp angles. It is less effective against teams that spike consistently. The players are not well situated to dig down-the-line or cross-court spikes. Coverage of the center deep area is also weak.

The most common defense in volleyball, by far, is the center-back defense. It, and its variations, are most effective against teams that spike consistently and powerfully. The following are variations of the center-back defense.

BASIC CENTER-BACK defense (fig 11.7) stations the center backrow (CB) player deep, near the end line. The left (LB) and right (RB) backcourt players are near their respective sidelines, in position to dig the down-the-line (RB) and cross-court (LB) spikes. The off-blocker (LF) moves away from the net to the 3-meter line.

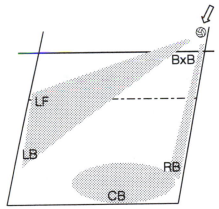

the basic center-back: FIG 11.7

The basic center-back does not require much movement; players start close to their digging positions. It is strong against both the cross-court and down-the line spikes. However, the down-the-line diggers are also responsible for covering tips. Unless the players can do both, the defense is vulnerable to teams that tip the ball well.

171

PERIMETER DEFENSE (fig 11.8) moves an additional player behind the block, providing additional coverage for balls driven deep over the block.

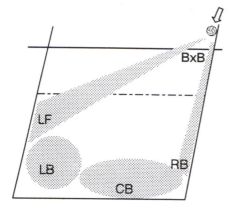

FIG 11.8: *perimeter defense*

When the set is made, the center back (CB) moves directly in line with the outside blocker. The cross-court player (LB) moves toward the corner, in line with the middle blocker. The off-blocker (LF) moves away from the net to dig the cross-court spike. The down-the-line digger covers the tip.

The outside blockers must be quick enough to move and dig the cross-court spike, and also help cover tips. The outside players must dig down-the-line spikes, and be quick enough to cover tips as well.

The perimeter defense is strong against balls driven over the block, or deep off of the blockers' hands. Teams with short blockers, for example, can benefit from this variation. however, like the basic center-back defense, it can be vulnerable to teams that tip well.

ROTATION DEFENSE (fig 11.9) is currently a popular defense, even though many teams using it lack the personnel to play it effectively. The rotation moves players into the seams of the coverage so that players cover two areas.

The rotation defense requires a great deal of movement in the backcourt. The down-the-line player (RB) moves up into the short tip area. The center back (CB), usually the best defensive player, moves towards the down-the-line area, but not quite all the way to the line. From here, they cover both the down-the-line spike and deep balls hit off the blockers.

The cross-court player (LB) moves toward the corner area, in the seam between the deep cross-court spike and the middle deep area. The off-blocker (LF) moves away from the net and covers the sharp cross-court spike.

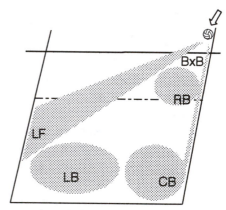

rotation defense: FIG 11.9

When played well, the rotation can be an effective defense. It requires a strong block, and good quickness in the backcourt. In many ways, it resembles the center-up defense (previous page). The rotation defense, however, is much more difficult to play because of the extensive player movement involved.

COUNTER-ROTATION DEFENSE (fig 11.10) is similar to the basic center-back defense. The backcourt players defend in the general area of their initial positions. The difference is that the off-blocker (LF) moves across the court to cover the tip.

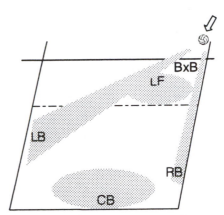

FIG 11.10: *the counter-rotation*

The down-the-line player (LB) digs the down-the-line spike. The cross-court players (RB) remains in position to dig cross-court spikes. The center back (CB) covers the deep area behind the block.

Though the counter-rotation is seldom used as a base defense, it can be effective as a situational defense, used only occasionally. The major disadvantage is that, once the ball is dug, the off blocker is far from his or her hitting position. Some hitters can overcome this and still hit effectively, others may not. Often, teams use their backcourt hitters to attack the area vacated by the off-blocker.

Keep in mind that there really is no 'BEST' defensive system. Teams should use the defensive scheme that best suits the abilities of their players.

Special Situations

During the course of a game special situations occur which require special adjustments from the defense. Among the more common of such situations are:
1)   fast middle attacks;
2)   single blocks against the outside attack;
3)   down ball situations;
4)   free ball situations.

A sound overall defensive strategy will address each of these situations, and any others that might normally occur in a match. In doing so, the defensive scheme defines the role of each player in making the necessary adjustments. What follows are examples of defensive coverages in the special situations listed above. Keep in mind that these are only examples. Each team makes adjustments based on their overall defensive strategy and personnel.

FAST MIDDLE ATTACKS   Strategies for blocking the middle attack vary from team to team. Some teams block with only one blocker (the middle blocker), others want to use two blockers. Against slow middle attacks, some teams block with all three blockers. Outside blockers seldom remain near the sideline area; they either block, or cover tips in the short area.

173

The backcourt defenders' play is coordinated with the blocker directly in front of them so that both the spike and the tip are covered.

In the example provided (fig 11.11), the left-side backrow player (LB) is responsible for digging spikes hit to the sideline area. If the left-side blocker blocks, the opposing hitter cannot spike the ball to the sideline; the blockers are in the way. The left-side backcourt player (LB) immediately moves forward and covers the short area.

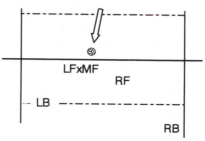

defense against the fast middle
FIG 11.11

The right-side backrow player (RB) is responsible for digging spikes hit to the right sideline area. If the right-side blocker (RF) DOES NOT block, the opposing hitter can spike the ball to the sideline; in this case, the blockers are not in the way. The right-side backcourt player (RB) remains back, in position to dig the spike that is open to the hitter. The right-side blocker (RB) covers the short area, instead.

ONE-ON-ONE ATTACKS   Ideally, the middle blocker always arrives at the point of attack in time to block alongside the outside blocker, giving the defense a double block. However, this is not always possible. Strong middle play by an opponent can delay the middle blocker; fast-tempo sets may beat the middle blocker to the outside. Occasionally, outside blockers must block alone, and defenses must cover a larger area of the court (fig 11.12).

The middle blocker (MF), too late to reach the attack and block, continues on to the outside and covers the short area. This allows all four backcourt players to play the anticipated spike. On typical sets, however, the outside blocker (RF) moves the block a little more inside, taking away the cross-court corner. The backcourt players divide the remaining court equally, two on each side of the blocker.

The off-blocker (LF) moves away from the net and digs the sharp cross-court spike. The cross-court player (LB) covers the larger cross-court area. On the other side of the blocker, the line player (RB) digs the down-the-line spike. The center-back player moves to the down-the-line side of blocker and covers that area. The key to the coverage is for the LB and CB to move so that the blocker is NOT between them and the hitter.

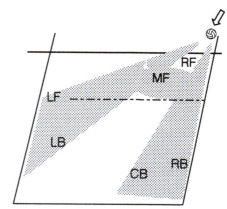

one-person block: FIG 11.12

174

It is much easier for spikers to hit the ball downward against a solo block than it is against a double block. Diggers, therefore, need to play about a step closer to the hitter than they normally do. Even with all these coverage adjustments, the hitter is still at a tremendous advantage; if is much preferable to have a double block.

NO BLOCK SITUATIONS   Occasionally, situations occur where the blockers should not block. There really are no hard rules that define when to block, and when not to block. It depends on a number of factors:
1)   the blockers' ability,
2)   the team's digging ability,
3)   the opposing hitter's ability,
4)   the location of the set.

A hitter who is standing flat footed on the ground, for example, is not much of a threat. Neither is a weak hitter spiking from 7-10 feet off the net. A strong hitter, however, can be very effective from this distance, especially if there is no block. The blockers must make a quick decision whether or not to block. The backcourt defense adjusts according to the blockers' decision.

FREE-BALL situations occur when
1)   the blockers decide not to block, AND
2)   they move away from the net into coverage positions.

Only when both outside blocker are in coverage can the backcourt players move into 'free-ball' coverage (fig 11.13).

The outside blockers, (LF) and (RF), move away from the net and cover the short areas, including the short middle. As the blockers move into position (not before), the setter (S) is free to move to the net in preparation to set. The backcourt players, (LB) and (RB) also adjust their positions as the blockers move into coverage. They move into deeper coverage, being especially aware of the area vacated by the setter.

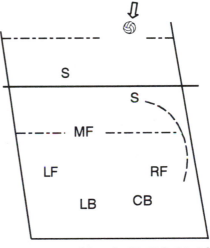

'free-ball': FIG 11.13

By the time the offense sends the ball across, each defender should be in position, and be in a balanced and stable posture. The overall coverage pattern will vary from team to team but, generally, it will resemble the team's serve receive formation.

DOWN-BALL situations (fig 11.14) occur when the blockers decide not to block at the last second, when it is too late to move into digging position. Without the middle (MF) and outside (RF) blockers moving into coverage, the backcourt players, (LB) and (CB), along with the off-blocker (LF) must cover the entire court. Included in the coverage is the area that was to have been blocked.

The setter (S) must also remain in coverage, instead of moving to the net. Even so, the court area is too large to cover. The defense's best hope is for a weak attack . . . which, of course, is why the blockers chose not to block in the first place.

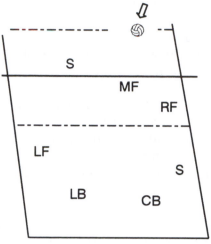

'down-ball': FIG 11.14

Transition

The defensive play does not end when the ball is dug. Along with digging the ball, the defense must make the transition to offense. It must convert the defensive play into an attack.

The first step in the transition is to control the dig, to pass the ball into an area from which the offense can run. Of course, the defensive system must have someone in that area who can set the ball.

Often, the setter's blocking and backcourt defensive positions are determined with the transition game in mind. Indeed, some teams design their entire defensive coverage so that the setter is in the best position to set in transition. That may be a little extreme, considering that they have to dig the ball before they can set in transition.

Generally, the setter is positioned on the right side. This allows the transition offense to run from the same area as the regular offense. Backcourt diggers direct the ball to the same place that they do when passing a serve. The transition offense, then, is very similar to the regular offense.

Before the ball is even dug, the blockers become hitters. They should move away from the net and get ready to spike. Once in position, the hitters can run special transition plays, or run the same offensive plays they regularly use.

APPENDIX A: DEFINITION of TERMS

Attack -- technically, any act which sends the ball over the net. Generally, it is an offensive play that 'attacks' the defense, such as a spike or tip.

Attack zones -- attack locations along the net as defined by the offense.

Back set -- a set directed back over the player's head, to a position behind the setter.

Block -- an attempt by the defense to prevent the ball from crossing the net.

Commit-block -- a blocking mode in which the blocker (usually a middle blocker) commits to blocking a fast-tempo attack by jumping when the spiker jumps, rather than waiting until the ball is set.

Cross-court -- toward the opposite sideline from the spiker.

Cross-over step -- a lateral movement pattern in which one foot crosses over in front of the other foot.

Dig -- the individual act of controllign and passing an opponent's spike.

Down-the-line -- toward the sideline nearest the spiker.

Floater serve -- a serve with no spin, causing the ball to 'floats' similar to a knuckleball in baseball.

Forearm pass -- a ball-handling technique in which the ball is rebounded from the forearms.

Goofy-footed (approach) -- a spike-approach pattern in which the last two steps are: nonhitting-hand foot, then hitting-hand foot side of the body.

High posture -- a body posture in which the player stands nearly upright.

Jumpset -- a set executed by a player who has jumped into the air.

Low posture -- a body posture in which the player plays very close to the floor.

Medium posture -- a body posture about half way in between low and upright.

Middle blocker -- a blocker who starts near the middle of the net area.

Off-hand side -- right side for a right-hander; left side for a left-hander.

On-hand side -- the left side for a right-hander; right side for a left-hander.

Outside blocker -- a blocker who starts nearer one of the sidelines.

Overhead technique) -- the act of playing a ball from head level or above, using finger action to control and direct the ball.

Pass -- the initial reception of a ball that is then directed to a teammate.

Passing platform -- the placement of the arms when rebounding the ball during the forearm pass.

Read-block -- a blocking mode in which the blocker (usually the middle blocker) sees the set first, then reacts and blocks that attack.

Second-tempo attack -- an attack in which the hitter is about one step from jumping as the set is delivered.

Set -- the act of placing the ball in position, by any means, for a spike. teammate to attack.

Side-out -- the exchange of service that occurs when the receiving team wins the play.

Slide step -- a lateral movement sequence in which the feet do not cross.

Spike -- the act of jumping and hitting the ball forcefully across the net.

Tempo -- the speed at which an attack takes place, usually determined by the height of the set.

Tip -- the act of jumping and sending the ball softly across the net, usually disguised as a spike.

Topspin -- the forward spin imparted to the ball, causing the ball to sink.

178